The TASTES of WASHINGTON

BY FRED BRACK & TINA BELL

Foreword by Bert Greene

Design by Elizabeth Watson

Published by the editors of *Washington* magazine

Evergreen Publishing Company, Seattle

*Published by Evergreen Publishing Company, Inc.,
200 W. Thomas, Suite 300, Seattle, Washington 98119*

*This book was printed in Japan by Dai Nippon
Printing Co., on 128 gsm paper. Color separations
and stripping were by Dai Nippon Printing Co. The
typestyle is Goudy Oldstyle, set 11 point on 13 point
leading on a Merganthaler Linotron 202.*

Library of Congress Cataloging in Publication Data
Brack, Fred, 1940-
    The tastes of Washington.

    "Published by the editors of Washington magazine."
    Includes index.
    1. Cookery, American.   2. Cookery—Washington (State)
I. Bell, Tina, 1938-   II. Title.
TX715.B794 1986   641.59797   86-80595
ISBN 0-937627-00-3

Second Printing 1987
Third Printing 1989

TABLE OF CONTENTS

FOREWORD

As any cook worth his (or her) salt will aver, *place determines taste.* Meaning, in the most rudimentary sense, that it is the happy accident of geography that causes an ingredient to be prime in the first place; which is, without question, the basis of any great dish.

At the outset, I must confess that I have *not* traveled the entire globe nor sampled all of its golden pickings on the spot. However, after peregrinations on at least three continents, I can state without equivocation that no produce–outranks the yield offered up in the Northwestern quadrangle of the United States. Specifically, the Evergreen State of Washington, which is a territory that has also offered up some of the most conspicuous chow I've ever consumed!

I suspect I am a mite prejudiced to things Washingtonian since, that territory is part of my own culinary heritage, albeit three generations removed. I am speaking of my paternal grandfather, who at age twelve was a "smithy's devil" during the Civil War, helping to repair worn muskets and learning to shoe the horses of the United States cavalry. When he attained his manhood, Michael Greene became a full-fledged blacksmith himself–an itinerant one–and crisscrossed the country in a covered wagon with a forge and bellows, spending the rest of his life in transit, fixing pots and pans and trimming equine hooves all the way from New York's South Ferry to Seattle's Puget Sound.

My father's tales of these westward treks were always somewhat dimly recollected for he was a small child when his own parents died. But he retained one spectacularly green memory (that was duly passed down to me) of a barrel of Washington State apples that had been transported intact from an orchard near the Columbia River to a tenement on Orchard Street in Manhattan's lower East Side, as a souvenir of his journey.

I never bit into a Washington State apple–on local turf–until 35 years after my own father's death, so at the very least a century had elapsed since my grandfather nibbled one there. And while the prodigious fruit was firmly rooted in family consciousness, I never realized until the very first meeting of tooth and tongue with Gravenstein and Newton Pippin what a taste connection existed between the terminal twig and trunk of my family tree.

Dare I admit more Greenelore? Though my Victorian parent never spoke of such things publicly, it was certainly private knowledge in the family that my bespoke grandfather made far too many excursions to Washington State in his Conestoga wagon for the route to be entirely coincidental. And there was always hushed talk of illegitimate progeny sired in alien corn that frankly inflamed my imagination as much as it blighted my father's.

On my very first trip to Seattle and Tacoma in the mid-1970s, I spent an entire morning poring over the telephone directory in my hotel, sifting through all of the Greenes listed there–hoping for the possibility of some Western kinsmen. Then, I addressed myself to more important matters at hand–and ate my first memorable meal in the area.

There may be a more tonic landscape than the mauve shadow of Mt. Rainier, floating disconnected above the clouds, in which to celebrate the genuine gifts of this universe (like Olympia oysters, Dungeness crab, Coho and King salmon or even a pearly-fleshed Russet Burbank baked potato awash with melting butter) but for the life of me, I cannot name one.

In time, the mind becomes surfeited with superlatives. I grew up hearing Washington State described (secondhand of course) as "God's Country," but never believing it for an instant–until the moment my eye surveyed the curious convergence of shoreline, treetop, field, stream and mountainside that is its overwhelming topography.

Or, more pertinently, since I am speaking of earthly pleasures here—until the very first swallow of dishes prepared from the gifts of both sea and soil still to be found there.

This book is a wondrous collection of all those gifts, carefully annotated and scrupulously transcribed.

I have never wolfed fresh asparagus from the Yakima Valley's mineral-rich stockpile, but Fred Brack and Tina Bell have certainly got me salivating at the prospect. Particularly when the green and savory spears rest under a jade coverlet (devised of more asparagus, cream and butter) that the authors have prescribed as its fitting complement. Similarly, I have not as yet consumed a golden onion in Walla Walla, nor pocketed a wild chanterelle or boletus mushroom on the Olympic Peninsula but, by gosh, after a long hard glance at this manual of their artful preparation, I certainly mean to.

The Tastes of Washington is a book obviously meant to whet the appetite in absentia; and in passing give readers in distant parts a reason (like the wild geese) to fly westward once a year.

Bert Greene

INTRODUCTION

Here we are, stuck up in the far left-hand corner of the United States of America, a long way from the corridors of political clout, the boardrooms of financial power and the control rooms of media decisions. To most of our countrymen, we live in a permanently shaded area on their TV weather map, and Mount St. Helens looms right above us all. We are Washingtonians, strangers to our own country.

We are America's best-kept secret.

Oh, yes, apples. You grow apples out there, don't you?

We sure do.

And salmon. You eat a lot of salmon. Right.

Gee, you're, um, lucky.

If only you knew.

If only you knew about the asparagus, the cherries, the raspberries and blueberries and cranberries and gooseberries, the oysters and crabs, apricots and peaches, clams and mussels, wild mushrooms, russet potatoes, Anjou and Bartlett pears, and the luscious onions from Walla Walla. If only you knew about the *geoduck*.

Then you'd know just how incredibly lucky we are. How we live in a state bursting with good things to eat, a state unimaginably bountiful.

That's what this book is about: How lucky we are. It was written by Washingtonians for Washingtonians, to crack open the door of the Evergreen State's well-stocked larder and look around.

The book began as a series of articles in *Washington* magazine. Those articles, more or less intact, are presented here. Our intention was not to be an encyclopedia of every food grown or harvested in our state, as any fan of, say, lentils or lingcod (Washington's big in both those areas) will notice immediately. But we did hope to cover a dozen of the more celebrated items in our cornucopia.

The idea was to help those people who become as excited as we do when local asparagus first appears in the market, when Walla Walla Sweets arrive again, as they do each July. And so on and on. Learning a little more about the foods that flourish in our state, where they come from, what they mean to our economy and how we can better enjoy them, and passing that information along, was our goal.

Beyond that, we wanted to offer, by way of enjoying recipes, some suggestions on this bounty once it reaches the kitchen.

Here we confronted a problem: how to make the recipes accessible to novice cooks while not overburdening knowledgeable cooks with detail on basic techniques. Our solution was to split the difference. Because that's inadequate, we ask everyone's indulgence and urge beginners, to brush up on basics in the best cookbook we know, *The Joy of Cooking*.

The recipes, however, are meant for the home cook, unlike so many cookery books that seem useful only to professional chefs with their elaborate equipment and ready access to exotic ingredients.

You will notice that the verb "process" appears here often. Food processors have become almost standard in avid cooks' kitchens. For those who don't possess one, in most cases we've suggested other methods of achieving the same result.

Finally, we urge the timid cook not to be intimidated by the ingredient lists or the preparation notes. No cook progresses without being assertive as to his or her own taste and ideas. The best result we could hope for in presenting these recipes would be to provoke cooks into developing their own variations.

We also hope that even those people who don't cook will enjoy this book by gaining a wider understanding of how lucky we are to live in Washington.

Fred Brack and Tina Bell
Seattle, Washington, 1986

NOTES ON INGREDIENTS

Balsamic vinegar: This mellow red vinegar from Italy is widely available in specialty food stores. Several recipes in *The Tastes of Washington* call for it. If it's not available, red wine vinegar may be substituted, although the taste will not be the same since balsamic is not fermented and therefore is not sour.

Butter: Though butter once was salted to preserve it, nowadays it's salted because Americans have grown accustomed to the taste. Salted and unsalted butter may be used interchangeably in the recipes presented here, although all were developed and tested with unsalted butter. In those recipes we think must have unsalted butter, we have specified it.

Cream: We have dropped the label "heavy" from recipes using cream because only light whipping cream is now widely available.

Creme fraiche: Here are two easy methods of preparing this thick, lightly cultured cream. (Unpasteurized cream is best.)

Mix 1 tablespoon buttermilk into 1 cup cream. Cover and let stand at room temperature 12-24 hours, until thick. Cream may be refrigerated after that for several days and will thicken further.

Or:

Whip 1 cup sour cream to incorporate air. Heat 1½ cups cream until lukewarm. Remove from heat and stir in sour cream. Cover and let stand at room temperature overnight, until thick. Cream may be refrigerated after that for several days and will thicken further.

Herbs: Fresh herbs are better, by far. When substituting dried for fresh, use half as much.

Parsley: Flat-leaf, "Italian" parsley has more flavor and is therefore more desirable than its cousin.

Pepper: Ground pepper quickly loses flavor. If possible, always use freshly ground.

Scallion: This is the term we've used for the vegetable also called "green onion."

Stock: Whether vegetable, meat or fish, quality stocks are essential to the final flavor of many dishes in this book. The home cook, however, often hasn't the time to prepare them. In the case of chicken, canned stock isn't too bad, especially if it's boiled down by about a third to concentrate flavor. In the case of beef, we suggest freshening canned stock using the following method devised by the late Michael Field, a food writer and cooking teacher:

Quarter 2 small onions (or 1 large). Brown the onions in 2 tablespoons butter. Add ¾ cup white wine to the pan and boil to reduce to ½ cup. Add 4 cups canned beef stock or bouillon, a chopped carrot, 2 peeled cloves of garlic, ½ teaspoon thyme, a bay leaf, some parsley and/or celery tops and, if available, the white part of a leek. Half-cover the pan and simmer 30-45 minutes. Strain before using.

If you have time, canned chicken stock can be freshened this way:

To 4 cups canned chicken stock, add 1 chopped onion, 1 chopped carrot, ½ chopped celery stalk, ½ bay leaf, ¼ teaspoon thyme, some parsley and, if available, the white part of a leek. Half-cover the pan and simmer 30-45 minutes. Strain before using.

Wine in cooking: Unless otherwise specified, always use dry wines for preparing recipes in this book. The better the wine, the better the dish. Especially when making a sauce that calls for wine, it's appropriate to use the wine the dish will be served with.

Zest: This term refers to the minced peel of a citrus fruit. When preparing zest, peel the fruit thinly, avoiding the bitter white pith underneath.

ACKNOWLEDGEMENTS

The authors' heartfelt thanks to:

Ken Gouldthorpe and Knute Berger, whose instant enthusiasm and support made this book possible.

Martin Rudow, David Fuller, Carrie Seglin, Elizabeth Watson, Jodi Pintler and Jayn Butt, whose devotion moved the book to completion.

Nick Allison, Diane Berger and Judy Gouldthorpe, whose yeoman copyediting and proofreading were exemplary.

Mark Burnside, David Lund and John Gallagher, whose artistry has illustrated our points.

The production artists, typesetters and fact-checkers at Evergreen Publishing Company, whose care dotted our i's and accented our sautés.

The friends and strangers who so willingly shared their recipes and kitchen secrets with us.

PHOTOGRAPHY CREDITS

COVER
  Mark Burnside
APPLES
  Mark Burnside, 1
  John Gallagher, 4
ASPARAGUS
  Mark Burnside, 13
  John Gallagher, 16
BERRIES
  Mark Burnside, 23
  Gary Greene, 26
BIVALVES
  Mark Burnside, 41
  Joel Rogers, 44
CHICKEN
  Charles Krebs, 53
  Phil Schofield, 56
CRAB
  Charles Krebs, 63
  John Gallagher, 66

MUSHROOMS
  Terry Pagos, 73
  Doug Plummer, 76
PEARS
  Oregon Washington
    California Pear Bureau, 85
  John Gallagher, 88
POTATOES
  Mark Burnside, 95
  John Gallagher, 98
SALMON
  Mark Burnside, 105
  John Gallagher, 108
STONE FRUIT
  Jim Mears/Northwest
    Cherry Growers, 117
  John Gallagher, 120
WALLA WALLAS
  Mark Burnside, 129
  John Gallagher, 132

APPLES

APPLES

A hundred yards or so from the north bank of the Columbia River in Vancouver, a lone apple tree stands amidst the arcs and curves of the interchange of the Lewis and Clark Highway and Interstate 5. Having survived for 160 years in the nation's leading apple-producing state, The Old Tree and its symbolism were powerful enough to stave off even the relentless thrust of concrete motorways.

Though its origin is a bit murky, the commonly accepted story is that The Old Tree was among the first apple trees planted in what would become Washington State. Its seed is believed to have been brought from England by Lt. Emilius Simpson of the Hudson's Bay Company in 1825. Sprouted in a greenhouse, Simpson's apple trees were transplanted to Fort Vancouver on the banks of the Columbia in 1826. From that first small orchard, only The Old Tree remains standing.

It would be nice to report that The Old Tree was the progenitor of Washington's enormous apple industry. It would be nice, but it would not be true. The truth is that Washington's preeminence in the apple business rests largely on a chance mutation that occurred in Jesse Hiatt's little orchard in Peru, Iowa, about 1870. Some 20 years later, a nurseryman bit into a strawberry-hued fruit from Hiatt's mutant tree and promptly drew from his hip pocket a little book in which he habitually jotted down prospective names for new fruit varieties. He knew just what he wanted to enter. "Delicious," he christened Hiatt's apple, thereby setting off a chain of events that would one day mean billions of dollars to the state of Washington.

Washington is the number-one apple producer in the US, growing over a third of the nation's apples. Fully one-half of all apples sold as fresh in this country are from Washington. That's five billion fresh apples per year. The most common variety, Red Delicious, which is descended from Hiatt's magic tree, accounts for nearly two-thirds of the crop and is a familiar sight in markets from Los Angeles to New York, from Taiwan to Saudi Arabia.

For the cook, however, the Red Delicious is irrelevant. It is not a cooking apple because it's too sweet, too dry and, some contend, has a corky aftertaste. Another leading Washington apple, the tangy Winesap, likewise is for eating fresh. Tart Yellow Pippins (also known as Newtown Pippins), however, are good pie apples, and the round Rome Beauty is widely considered the world's best baking apple.

The latter two are not especially important commercial apples in Washington. But the state's second most important commercial apple, the Golden Delicious variety,

APPLE-CABBAGE SAUTÉ WITH MEDALLIONS OF PORK

This is a city version of a farm-house dish, especially appropriate on cool autumn evenings. The two parts of this recipe are prepared separately, then combined at the last minute.

Apple-Cabbage Sauté

    ½ cup shallots, minced
    4 tablespoons duck fat or butter
    1 medium green cabbage, shredded
        coarsely
    Salt and pepper
    2 medium apples, peeled, cored
        and chopped coarsely
    2 tablespoons balsamic vinegar

1. Sauté shallots in duck fat (or butter) 5 minutes without browning. Add cabbage and sauté at low heat for 20 minutes. Salt and pepper to taste.
2. Add apples and continue cooking for another 20 minutes, until cabbage is limp and has shrunk in volume. Add vinegar to taste and cover skillet to keep warm.

Medallions of Pork

    1 pound pork tenderloin, trimmed of fat
    Salt and pepper
    Flour
    8 tablespoons butter
    ¼ cup strong chicken or veal stock
    1¼ cups cream
    ¼ cup Madeira
    2 tablespoons Dijon-style mustard

1. Cut medallions diagonally about ½ inch thick. Pound lightly between sheets of waxed paper. Salt and pepper to taste and dredge lightly in flour.
2. In 6 tablespoons of the butter, brown medallions over medium-high heat 1 minute on each side. Transfer to a heated platter and keep warm.

3. Add stock, cream and Madeira to pan juices and reduce by half over medium-high heat. Stir in mustard and remaining butter.
4. Pour sauce over pork and serve immediately with apple-cabbage mixture.

Serves 4-6

APPLE SALAD

Betsy Sestrap, marketing director of Wax Orchards on Vashon Island, is an apple fancier for more than professional reasons, though her family's firm produces some of the best apple ciders, juices and butters in the Northwest. Chopped apples shouldn't be overlooked as a salad ingredient, she notes, and she offers this recipe as proof. Golden Delicious is her choice as a salad apple because of its balance between sweetness and tartness.

    3 cups coarsely chopped Nappa cabbage
    ½ cup mayonnaise
    2 tablespoons milk
    2 cups apples, diced
    2 tablespoons finely chopped onion
    ½ stalk celery, sliced thinly

1. Place chopped cabbage in a large bowl. In a smaller bowl, mix mayonnaise with milk to thin, then add apples, stirring to coat them. Add onion and mix.
2. Mix celery with cabbage, and then blend in the apple-mayonnaise mixture. Let flavors blend for 1 hour at room temperature before serving.

Serves 4-6

Wilma Tolley of Dixie dicing apples.

which constitutes about one-quarter of the crop, also has a reputation as a decent cooking apple.

Golden Delicious, though it has a similar shape, is related to Red Delicious in name only. As a cooking apple, it has several positive attributes. Its slices hold their shape well under heat, a plus for those who like to see as well as taste apples in pies, and a must in sautéing or poaching. Its skin is tender so it does not have to be peeled for, say, salads or applesauce. And its flesh remains white after cutting so it does not have to be plunged into acidulated water between preparing and cooking and still looks inviting after sautéing.

Golden Delicious is an all-around apple because of its balance between sweet and sour. For some tastes, it's too sweet, but that objection can be partly overcome by selecting greener apples. On the other hand, it's also possible to make applesauce from Goldens without having to add sugar. Finally, though, the Golden Delicious has one drawback as a cooking apple: its flavor is too mild for many tastes.

A better choice for cooking is the green Granny Smith, fast gaining popularity

APPLE AND PORK STEW

The spicy tang of fresh hard cider makes this dish an autumnal treat.

> 2½ pounds boneless pork,
>   cubed and defatted
> 1 teaspoon salt
>   Pepper
> 2 tablespoons minced fresh rosemary
>   (or 2 teaspoons dried)
> 1 cup flour
> 2 tablespoons butter
> 2 tablespoons vegetable oil
> 1 cup sliced onions
> 4 cloves garlic, chopped
> 1 cup meat stock
> 2 cups hard cider
> 1 tablespoon Dijon-style mustard
> 1 pound turnips, peeled and cubed
> 1 pound apples, peeled and cut into
>   eighths
> 1 cup cream

1. Rub pork with salt, pepper and 1 tablespoon rosemary. Marinate for a day in refrigerator.
2. Pat dry. Dredge in flour, shaking off excess. In heavy skillet, brown pork over medium-high heat in butter and oil. When finished, turn down heat to medium and brown onions and garlic lightly in skillet with pork. Remove all to casserole.
3. Pour off fat from skillet, turn up heat, add stock and boil to reduce by one-half. Add cider, bring to boil, scraping up brown bits from skillet. Add mustard and remaining tablespoon of rosemary and stir.
4. Salt turnips and apples. Combine with pork in casserole, pour liquid from skillet over all, cover casserole and bake at 325°F for 50 minutes to 1 hour, until pork is tender.
5. Remove pork from casserole, along with half the apple and turnip pieces. Degrease juices. Mash apples and turnips remaining in casserole into the juices, or process together. Add cream, pork and reserved apple and turnip pieces. Reheat.

Serves 4-6

APPLE-TURNIP PUREE

This goes well with any main dish that will not suffer from the slightly sweet taste of the puree.

> ½ cup chopped onion
> 6 tablespoons butter
> 1 pound young turnips, peeled and cubed
> 2 medium apples, peeled, cored
>   and chopped coarsely
>   Salt and white pepper
> ¼ cup cream, scalded
> 2 tablespoons minced parsley

1. Sauté onions in butter over low heat for 10 minutes, without browning them. Add turnips and apples. Continue sautéing for 15 minutes or until tender. Salt and pepper to taste.
2. Transfer mixture to food processor and process until smooth (or mash and whip by hand). Add cream and process well until combined. (If too stiff, add more cream slowly.)
3. Stir in parsley and serve immediately, or reheat over low heat in a frying pan. The puree can also be kept warm in a 200°F oven, covered with foil and a heavy lid to keep it from drying out.

Serves 4-6

among Washington orchardists. Granny Smith is an aromatic apple with the requisite sourness for cooking.

But there are some other excellent choices. Oddly, these are found *west* of the Cascades, although the commercial apple business is situated almost entirely east of the mountains. Delicious, both Red and Golden, Winesap and Granny Smith are hot-weather apples, ideal crops for Eastern Washington's valleys. The colder, moister conditions west of the Cascades don't favor these varieties and lead to a fungus in them called "scab." Other varieties, fortunately, thrive in Western Washington. The Washington apple business actually began on the west side, principally in Clark County and the San Juan Islands. But by 1890, five years after the Northern Pacific Railway entered the Yakima Valley, the apple industry had decisively moved east of the mountains.

Today there is a resurgent interest in growing apples commercially in Western Washington. A number of varieties are being developed specifically to meet the growing conditions of the western part of the state. All are "dual-purpose" apples, suitable for eating fresh and for cooking. "We have homely apples in Western Washington," one man involved in testing these varieties said. "They don't have as brilliant a finish as Eastern Washington apples and tend toward 'russeting' (a brown, blistering skin condition). But they are terrific tasting, and lots of old-timers actually prize russet apples."

Foremost among Western Washington apples is the Gravenstein, different types of which are either green or yellow, often with a blush. Gravenstein is the ideal sauce apple. Its skin is tender enough to be left on, its texture is fluffy and its taste is tart and fresh. Gravenstein fanciers are even more enthusiastic about a relatively new apple being grown in Washington called Jonagold, or, as the name is often corrupted, Johnnygold. A cross between a Jonathan and a Golden Delicious, the Jonagold is excellent for pies, with a Jonathan's tartness and a Golden Delicious' capacity to hold its shape.

Unlike Eastern Washington apples, west-side varieties tend not to store well. The Red and Golden Delicious and Granny Smiths found in markets in the spring all come from "controlled-atmosphere" storage, where they are sealed in cool rooms with reduced oxygen.

The accompanying recipes do not specify apple varieties, largely because their availability is seasonal and many are interchangeable. Use the Washington variety you prefer, remembering to alter the amount of sugar called for according to the apple used.

APPLE-HAM PATÉ

Serve this cold as a lunch dish or a first course for dinner. As a condiment, try blueberry chutney (see page 29), cranberry ketchup (see page 35) or mustard sauce below.

    5 prunes, pitted and chopped coarsely
    ½ cup Port
    1 pound boneless pork
    ½ pound boneless veal
    ½ pound fatback
    ⅓ cup apple brandy
    1 tablespoon butter
    ¼ cup minced onion
    2 cloves garlic, minced
    2 medium apples, peeled and cored
    2 teaspoons salt
    1 teaspoon pepper
    ½ teaspoon allspice
    ¼ teaspoon nutmeg
    2 eggs, lightly beaten
    ½ cup cream
    ½ pound sliced bacon
    ¼ pound smoked ham, cut into
        ¼-inch-square strips

1. Soak prunes in Port 1 hour.
2. Grind pork, veal and fatback together in processor or grinder. Mix brandy and prune-Port mixture into ground meat. Refrigerate 1 hour.
3. Sauté onion and garlic in butter over medium-low heat 10 minutes. Combine with meat mixture. Cut apples into small dice. Add to meat mixture along with seasonings. Combine eggs and cream and stir into meat mixture.
4. Sauté a bit of mixture and taste for seasoning, correcting if necessary.
5. Blanch bacon by placing in cold water, bringing to boil and simmering 5 minutes. Drain, rinse and pat dry.
6. Line buttered paté or loaf pan with bacon strips, crosswise, allowing ends to overhang. Reserve 3 slices for top. Smoothly layer about 1 inch of meat mixture over bacon strips, then press ham strips lengthwise into mixture, making 4 clean rows. Repeat with another layer of meat mixture and another 4 rows of ham strips. Top with remaining meat mixture. Arrange reserved bacon strips lengthwise on pate, flipping overhanging bacon strips over the top.
7. Cover with foil. If using paté pan, place lid on foil. Place pan in larger pan and pour in boiling water until it reaches halfway up sides of paté pan. Bake at 300°F for 2 hours.
8. Remove foil and bake about 30 minutes more, until center of paté registers 165°F on meat thermometer. Remove paté pan to rack for 1 hour to cool. Re-cover with the foil and, using a block of wood or any other flat surface that fits inside paté pan, weigh paté down with heavy cans. Refrigerate overnight.
9. Remove weights and age paté in refrigerator 2-4 days before serving. Serve paté either from the pan or unmold before slicing.

Serves 10-12

Mustard Sauce

    2 egg yolks
    2 cloves garlic, minced
    1 teaspoon Worcestershire sauce
    2 tablespoons Dijon-style mustard
    1 teaspoon salt
    1 cup olive oil
        Pepper
    ½ cup grated Parmesan

1. Process egg yolks, garlic, Worcestershire sauce, mustard and salt 1 minute. With machine running, slowly add olive oil, a few drops at a time at first and then in a thin, steady stream.
2. Add pepper to taste and stir in grated Parmesan.

7

APPLE CREAM PIE

Here's an easy variation on the traditional apple pie.

Pastry

1¼ cups flour
½ teaspoon salt
½ teaspoon cinnamon
¼ cup sugar
1 teaspoon baking powder
2 teaspoons lemon zest
4 ounces butter
1 egg yolk
2 tablespoons dry sherry

Filling

2 eggs
½ cup sugar
2 tablespoons flour, sifted
2 teaspoons lemon zest
½ cup cream
8 ounces cream cheese, softened
¼ cup seedless raisins, chopped coarsely
¼ teaspoon salt
2 medium apples, peeled, cored and sliced thinly

Topping

½ pint cream, whipped
1 teaspoon cinnamon

1. Prepare pastry by sifting together dry ingredients. Sprinkle with lemon zest, then cut in butter. Beat egg yolk with sherry and mix with flour mixture to form smooth ball. Cover with waxed paper and chill for up to 1 hour, so that pastry rolls out better.
2. For filling, beat eggs with sugar until thick. Gradually add flour while beating. Add lemon zest, cream, cream cheese, raisins and salt. Mix.
3. Roll out pastry to cover bottom of pie plate or shallow cake pan about 11 inches by 8 inches. Trim edges.
4. Arrange apple slices in an overlap pattern on pastry, cover with filling, smooth the top and bake at 350°F for about an hour.
5. Serve warm with whipped cream mixed with cinnamon, or serve cold, topping with whipped cream and sprinkled cinnamon.

Serves 6-8

APPLE-PEAR CHUTNEY

What could celebrate Washington's autumn fruit season better than this blend? Serve it with poultry, pork and lamb.

1 quart cider vinegar
3 cups sugar
6 pounds apples, peeled, cored and sliced into eighths
½ pound seedless raisins
2 medium heads garlic, peeled and slivered
½ pound fresh ginger, peeled and shredded
6 canned chiles, seeded and slivered
2 tablespoons salt
Cayenne pepper
6 pounds pears, peeled, cored and sliced into eighths
1 pound walnut halves

1. In a large, noncorrosive pan, combine 3 cups of the vinegar with the sugar. Boil for about 20 minutes, until syrupy.
2. Add remaining vinegar, apples, raisins, garlic, ginger, chiles, salt and cayenne to taste. Bring to boil, reduce heat and simmer 10 minutes.
3. Add pears and simmer until both pears and apples are cooked but not disintegrated. Stir in walnuts.
4. Cool and refrigerate or preserve according to your normal canning procedure.

Makes 6 pints

STEAMED APPLE PUDDING

This is a dandy holiday pudding, which can be made several months in advance and kept in the refrigerator. Refrigerate at least two weeks. This recipe makes two one-quart puddings.

> 1 cup raisins
> 1 cup coarsely chopped candied citron
> 1 cup coarsely chopped walnuts
> 1 cup brandy
> 8 tablespoons unsalted butter
> 1 cup firmly packed brown sugar
> 2 cups milk, scalded
> ½ cup instant tapioca
> 2 teaspoons baking soda
> 1 cup flour
> 2 cups dried bread crumbs
> ½ teaspoon cinnamon
> ¼ teaspoon nutmeg
> ⅛ teaspoon ground cloves
> 1 teaspoon salt
> 2 eggs, beaten
> 2 tablespoons molasses
> 2 apples, peeled and grated coarsely
>   Grand Marnier sauce (see below)

1. Soak raisins, citron and walnuts in brandy at least 2 hours at room temperature. (Overnight is better.)
2. Melt butter over low heat. Stir in brown sugar and melt. Remove from heat and stir in scalded milk until sugar is completely dissolved. Add tapioca and baking soda. Then let tapioca soften 20 minutes as the mixture cools.
3. Mix together flour, bread crumbs, cinnamon, nutmeg, cloves and salt. Stir in milk mixture, beaten eggs, molasses and the brandied fruit mixture. Stir in grated apples.
4. Turn batter into 2 buttered 1-quart pudding molds. (Place any extra batter in a smaller mold, such as a little bowl or large glass.) Secure lids (or cover with foil secured by string). Place in deep pan. Pour boiling water into pan until it reaches two-thirds up sides of molds. Cover pan and steam puddings over medium-low heat 2 hours.
5. Remove molds from steamer and cool. While still warm, however, prick puddings with skewer and pour more brandy over them. Once cooled, cover and refrigerate. (The brandy bath may be repeated as often as desired during refrigeration.)
6. Before serving, steam puddings 90 minutes to reheat. Serve warm with Grand Marnier sauce.

Each pudding serves 6-8

Grand Marnier Sauce

> 4 egg yolks
> ½ cup sugar
> ¾ cup cream
> ¼ teaspoon vanilla
>   Dash salt
> 1 cup milk, scalded
> 3 tablespoons Grand Marnier

1. Simmer water in the bottom of a double boiler.
2. Beat egg yolks with sugar in a bowl until the sugar is entirely dissolved and the mixture becomes light-colored and fluffy. Stir in cream, vanilla and salt. Gradually beat in scalded milk. Transfer mixture to the top of the double boiler, making certain top does not touch water.
3. Whisk constantly until the mixture thickens to the point that it coats the back of a spoon, about 5 minutes. Do not allow the mixture to boil. Remove from heat, stir in Grand Marnier and serve warm over apple pudding.

APPLE CHARLOTTE

A classic French dessert form, this charlotte glorifies homemade applesauce. The secret is to cook the applesauce until it's quite thick.

5 cups applesauce
3 tablespoons butter
¼ cup dark rum
1 loaf firm, slightly stale
    white bread, sliced
1 cup melted butter, clarified

1. Combine applesauce, butter and rum in heavy saucepan. Over medium-high heat, stirring frequently, cook mixture 15-20 minutes uncovered to let moisture evaporate and to allow applesauce to thicken.
2. Remove crusts from about 15 slices of bread. Select a straight-sided, round baking pan, soufflé dish or charlotte mold, with a capacity of 4-6 cups. To cover the bottom with bread, lay out 4 slices in a square, place pan on top of them and cut around to yield 4 wedges that will fit snugly into bottom of pan. Repeat to get wedges that will fit on top later.
3. In skillet, brown all 8 wedges lightly in some of the melted butter. Place 4 wedges in bottom of pan.
4. Cut remaining slices of bread into 2-inch strips, dip them in melted butter and stand them up, overlapping, around inside of pan.
5. Pack applesauce into mold in 3 layers. Cut unused strips of bread into pieces, dip them in butter and place a few between layers of applesauce. Pour on the remaining butter, then top with browned wedges to form lid.
6. Bake 30-40 minutes at 425°F, until bread strips around outside are browned. Upend pan onto serving plate and let stand 30 minutes before unmolding. It should unmold itself, but you might have to run a knife between bread strips and inside of pan. Serve warm with lightly whipped cream, sweetened to taste.

Serves 6

BAKED APPLE PANCAKE

Seattle actress and television host Pat Finley delights guests with this enticing dessert. It does take the cook away from the table. If that's a problem, serve it as a special breakfast.

Batter

8 eggs
1 cup flour
2 tablespoons sugar
1 teaspoon baking powder
  Pinch salt
2 cups milk
4 tablespoons butter, melted
2 teaspoons vanilla
¼ teaspoon nutmeg

Topping

2-3 cooking apples
8 tablespoons butter, melted
1 teaspoon cinnamon
1 cup sugar
¼ teaspoon nutmeg

1. Prepare batter by combining eggs, flour, sugar, baking powder, salt and milk. Mix until smooth. Blend in melted butter, vanilla and nutmeg. Let batter stand overnight in refrigerator or 30-40 minutes at room temperature.
2. Prepare topping by peeling, coring and thinly slicing apples. You should have two cups. Brush bottom and sides of heavy 10-inch skillet with half the melted butter. (Or, using two skillets, make two pancakes at once.) Combine cinnamon, sugar and nutmeg and sprinkle ¼ of mixture over butter in skillet. Layer 1 cup apple slices evenly over skillet bottom. Sprinkle apples with another ¼ of sugar-cinnamon mixture.
3. Place skillet over medium-high heat until mixture bubbles. Slowly pour half the batter over apples. Place skillet in 425°F oven and bake 15 minutes. Reduce heat to 375°F and bake another 10 minutes. Cut into 3 wedges and serve immediately.

Makes 2 pancakes or 6 servings

APPLE TART

This is a classic from Normandy.

1½ pounds apples, peeled, cored and sliced
2 tablespoons apple brandy
6 tablespoons sugar
⅛ teaspoon cinnamon
1 9-inch tart shell (see below)
3 egg yolks
1 cup crème fraiche (see Notes on
*   Ingredients, page xi)*
¼ cup slivered almonds
*   Unsweetened lightly whipped cream*

1. Soak apple slices for 1 hour in apple brandy mixed with 2 tablespoons of the sugar and the cinnamon. Drain and reserve liquid.
2. Spread apples in tart shell and bake at 350°F for 30 minutes.
3. Whip egg yolks with crème fraiche (or ordinary cream), 2 tablespoons of the sugar and reserved brandy-sugar mixture. Pour over apples in tart shell. Sprinkle with slivered almonds and the remaining sugar. Bake at 425°F for 15 minutes. Serve warm with whipped cream.

Serves 4-6

Tart Shell

1½ cups flour
1½ tablespoons sugar
*   Pinch salt*
2 teaspoons lemon juice
1 egg yolk
10 tablespoons unsalted butter, chilled
*   and cut into bits*
2-3 tablespoons ice water

1. Combine flour, sugar and salt in processor and process until mixed. Add lemon juice and egg yolk and process to blend. Add butter and process until mixture breaks into pea-size bits. Add ice water a little at a time until dough masses around blade.
2. Remove dough from processor and form into ball. Cover with plastic wrap and chill until firm, about 30 minutes. (Dough may be frozen and brought to room temperature before rolling out.)
3. For above recipe, roll out enough dough to cover 9-inch tart pan with removable rim. Press dough into flutes on rim and trim along rim top.
4. Prick shell all over with fork. Line shell with waxed paper and fill paper with dried beans or rice. Bake at 350°F for 15 minutes. Remove beans or rice and waxed paper. Bake about 15 minutes more, until shell is pale gold. Cool on rack. Brush with syrup made by dissolving 3 tablespoons sugar in 2 tablespoons water and boiling 5 minutes, brushing crystals from sides of pan as syrup cooks.
5. Return shell to hot oven for no more than 5 minutes to set.

APPLE AND HORSERADISH SAUCE

In Central Europe, this accompanies boiled beef. Use it with roasts, also.

1 cup applesauce
1 teaspoon sugar
*   Dash lemon juice*
2 tablespoons freshly grated horseradish

Mix ingredients and adjust seasonings.

Note: *Prepared horseradish can be substituted for fresh, though the sauce is not as good. One variation is to use prepared pink horseradish, which contains pickled beets.*

APPLE MOUSSE WITH PRALINE

The inclusion of hazelnut praline transforms this mousse.

> 2 pounds apples, peeled, cored
>   and sliced thinly
> 2 tablespoons butter
> 4 tablespoons brown sugar
> 1 teaspoon lemon zest
>   Pinch salt
> 1/8 teaspoon cinnamon
> 1 tablespoon unflavored gelatin
> 2 tablespoons cold water
> 4 eggs, separated
> 1/2 cup sugar
> 3 tablespoons apple brandy
> 1 1/2 cups cream
> 1 cup hazelnut praline (see below)

1. Make applesauce by cooking apple slices with butter and brown sugar over medium heat, stirring frequently, until no liquid remains. Mash. (You'll need 1 1/2 cups applesauce.) Add lemon zest, salt and cinnamon. Cool.
2. Soften gelatin in the cold water. Dissolve by placing container holding gelatin in pan of simmering water. Simmer, stirring, until dissolved. Stirring, add dissolved gelatin in slow stream to the applesauce.
3. Whip egg yolks with sugar until pale and thickened. Stir in apple brandy.
4. Whip cream until stiff. Clean beaters and whip egg whites until stiff but not dry.
5. Stir egg yolk-sugar mixture into applesauce. Fold in whipped cream and egg whites until blended. Fold in 1/2 cup of the praline.
6. Pour into mousse mold. Sprinkle with remaining praline. Refrigerate until set. Serve chilled.

Serves 4-6

Praline

> 1 1/4 cups hazelnuts (or blanched almonds)
> 1/2 cup sugar
> 2 tablespoons water

1. Spread hazelnuts in single layer on baking sheet and toast in 350°F oven 8-10 minutes. Rub nuts in towel to remove skins.
2. Boil sugar and water in small pan, swirling occasionally, until sugar turns nut-brown and is caramelized, about 3-4 minutes. Stir in hazelnuts. Bring to boil. Pour onto oiled baking sheet.
3. When cool, break mass into pieces and grind to coarse powder in processor or blender.

APPLE-CHILE RELISH

This zesty condiment goes with any roast pork or fowl.

> 1/2 cup raisins
> 2 cloves garlic, minced
> 4 apples, peeled, cored and chopped
> 1 onion, sliced
> 2 tablespoons vegetable oil
> 8 ounces canned green chiles
> 4 tablespoons white wine vinegar
> 1 tablespoon brown sugar
>   Salt and pepper
>   Pinch cayenne

1. Soak raisins in hot water 30 minutes to soften and plump.
2. Sauté garlic, apples and onion in oil over low heat until onions are soft. Seed chiles and cut into thin strips. Combine all remaining ingredients with apple-onion mixture and simmer until thick, 15-20 minutes. Cool, chill and serve.

Makes about 2 cups

ASPARAGUS

13

ASPARAGUS

E very region has its own special harbinger of spring. None is more glorious than that of Central Washington, where the season of renewal is heralded by fat fingers of asparagus pushing up through sandy soil.

The ancient Greeks and Romans would have envied Washingtonians. They regarded asparagus with a sort of awe, prizing its gustatory qualities and attributing to it all manner of medicinal value. So precious was asparagus to the Romans, in fact, that they grew it in high-walled courtyards.

Not only the Romans protected their asparagus from common marauders. For most of the 2,500 years this member of the lily family has been cultivated, asparagus was reserved for the wealthy and noble. Only in modern times has asparagus been widely available to ordinary people and priced within their reach.

In this country, Washington has had a lot to do with the asparagus boom. Some 32,000 acres of Central Washington land, mainly in the Yakima Valley, the Columbia Basin and the Walla Walla area, are devoted to asparagus. Only California can rival Washington when it comes to asparagus acreage and production. Each state grows about 30 percent of the country's crop.

There are differences, however. California's crop appears sooner, in early March. By the time Washington's begins poking its head above ground in mid-April, California has captured much of the country's fresh market. About 60 percent of Washington's crop, therefore, is canned or frozen. Asparagus fanciers know that either preservation method is no way to treat asparagus.

Fortunately, Washingtonians can procure ample supplies of their own state's crop fresh from the farm, and they seem to prefer it. This is due partly to climate, partly to soil. Central Washington is ideal for asparagus on both counts, with cold winters for a good "set" and light, mineral-rich soil.

Washington's commercial asparagus crop is all green. White reaching the market here usually comes from Mexico, where labor is cheaper. White asparagus and green asparagus are the same plant, but growing the former is more labor-intensive since the spears must be protected from sunlight by mounding soil around them or carefully picked by cutting them below ground.

Thin green asparagus seems to be gaining favor in this country, much to the despair of true asparagus lovers. Asparagus growers say many people believe that thin asparagus is more tender. Actually, the opposite is true. Asparagus begins to develop fibers from the moment it is picked. Given the same interval between harvest and table, a thin spear will be more fibrous relative to its volume than a thick spear.

Thin spears also signify that they have

ASPARAGUS PANE RIPIENO

"Stuffed bread" in English, *pane ripieno* is a superb appetizer or hot buffet item with an Italian accent. The choice of fillings is vast. Here it's done with asparagus, Fontina cheese and the Italian bologna, mortadella. This recipe makes two breads. The second can be frozen if the recipe is too much. (See note below.)

> 1 recipe dough (see below)
> 2 tablespoons olive oil
> ½ pound mortadella, sliced very thinly
> ½ pound Fontina cheese, sliced very
>   thinly
> 1½ pounds asparagus, peeled, barely
>   cooked and cooled
> 6 cured black olives, chopped finely
> 1 tablespoon minced fresh herbs
>   (optional)
> 2 tablespoons grated Parmesan
> 1 egg yolk
> 2 teaspoons water

1. Split dough in half. Proceed with each of the halves as below, making two stuffed breads.
2. Roll out dough to make rectangle 10 inches by 14 inches, with long dimension nearest you.
3. Brush dough with 1 tablespoon of the olive oil, oiling to edge only at bottom of rectangle and leaving 2-inch unoiled border on other 3 sides.
4. Beginning at oiled edge of bottom, lay on half the mortadella slices, overlapping each row. Cover only three-quarters of the dough, leaving top one-quarter and unoiled border on two short sides free of filling. Cover mortadella with cheese slices.
5. Make 3 or 4 long rows of asparagus (depending on spears' thickness) across cheese. Do not crowd. Then sprinkle on half the olives, half the optional fresh herbs and 1 tablespoon of the Parmesan.
6. Beat egg yolk with water to make wash. Brush unoiled border of dough with wash.

7. Fold up bottom of dough (with its filling) to reach middle of filling, without stretching dough. Roll over once like jellyroll. Fold over flap of unfilled top to complete package. Press gently to seal seam. Fold up end flaps and press gently to seal.
8. Gently flip roll seam-side down onto baking sheet that has been oiled and sprinkled with cornmeal. Brush top with egg wash. With knife tip, form 4 small steam vents down middle of roll and 4 on each side.
9. Bake at 400°F for 15 minutes. Cool 10 minutes before slicing and serving.

Each bread serves 4-6

Note: *If planning to freeze, bake at 400°F for 10 minutes. Cool. Wrap in foil and freeze. Later, defrost to room temperature. Bake at 450°F for 5-7 minutes, until outside is browned and contents are heated.*

Pane Ripieno Dough

> 1 package dry yeast
>   Pinch sugar
> ½ cup hot water
> 3 cups flour
> ¾ cup cold milk
> 1 teaspoon salt
> 2 tablespoons vegetable oil

1. Dissolve yeast and sugar in hot water. Pour flour into processor bowl and, with machine running, add yeast mixture, milk, salt and oil. Process until dough masses around blade. If more milk is needed, add it bit by bit. (By hand, mix ingredients in bowl and proceed as below.)
2. Turn out dough on floured board and let rest 5-10 minutes. Knead by hand for 8-10 minutes, until dough is soft and smooth.
3. Place dough in lightly oiled bowl, turning it over to coat top, and let rise, covered, 70-90 minutes, until doubled in bulk. Punch dough down. Turn dough out on lightly floured board, punch down, divide in half and form two balls. Let them rest 10-15 minutes before rolling out to make *pane ripieno*.

Jeffrey P. Bixby sampling Yakima Valley asparagus.

come from older, weaker plants, or that they are the plant's final effort of the season. A healthy asparagus plant at the peak of its performance naturally produces thick spears. Knowledgeable consumers, then, look for medium-to-thick spears, with firm, straight stalks and closed, compact heads. Limp stalks with loose heads are old asparagus, deficient in flavor and high in fiber.

Cooking asparagus is as easy as boiling water. Start by selecting stalks of uniform thickness so they will cook evenly. Rinse the stalks thoroughly under cold running water, paying particular attention to the heads, where grit may lurk. Next, snap off the woody ends by bending each spear until it breaks naturally. (The butts can be used for soup or flavoring stews.) Peeling asparagus is a matter of personal preference. Since fibers develop from the outside in, a few quick whisks with a vegetable peeler will eliminate most of the fiber from stalks that are not fresh from the farm.

Finally, cook the asparagus in boiling water, steam, or a combination, but do not overcook. Classically, asparagus is cooked in a tied bundle standing upright in several inches of water. A special asparagus cooker is ideal for this, but a covered coffeepot or any tall, narrow pot with a lid will do. The lid is necessary to keep in the steam, which cooks the tender bud-ends more slowly than the boiling water cooks the thick butt-ends. A skillet is excellent, too. Arrange the asparagus in a single layer, pour boiling water over to cover, pop on a lid and simmer. Cooking time varies with the method used and the thickness of the stalks. Ten minutes is about the maximum.

As an aristocrat among vegetables, asparagus needs little adornment. Melted butter, perhaps a drizzle of lemon juice, and salt and pepper are about all hot asparagus requires. Room-temperature or cold asparagus is excellent in a simple vinaigrette. Other saucings serve asparagus well, too, so long as they don't overwhelm the vegetable's flavor.

ASPARAGUS-GORGONZOLA SOUFFLÉ

This soufflé is enriched by the pungency of the Italian blue cheese. Served on a platter, it makes a dramatic presentation.

½ cup minced onion
10 tablespoons butter
2 cups asparagus pieces, peeled and barely cooked
5 tablespoons flour
1½ cups milk, scalded
Salt and pepper
5 egg yolks
⅔ cup crumbled Gorgonzola cheese
7 egg whites
2 tablespoons grated Parmesan

1. Sauté onion in 2 tablespoons of the butter 2-3 minutes over medium-low heat. Sauté asparagus pieces with onions 8-10 minutes, until quite tender. Puree in processor, blender or food mill.
2. Prepare béchamel by melting remaining butter in small pan over low heat. When it stops foaming, beat in flour and cook, stirring, 2 minutes without allowing to color. Remove from heat and pour in scalded milk all at once, beating to blend. Return pan to medium-high heat and, stirring, bring to boil. Boil 2-3 minutes, stirring constantly. Salt and pepper to taste. Allow to cool.
3. When béchamel is cooled, beat in egg yolks and Gorgonzola. Stir in asparagus puree.
4. Whip egg whites until they form firm peaks. Stir a third of them into asparagus mixture, then fold remainder into mixture until barely combined. Do not overmix.
5. Butter a 12-inch platter or shallow baking dish and sprinkle with half the Parmesan. Pour soufflé mixture into dish and sprinkle with remaining Parmesan. Bake at 375°F for 15 minutes, reduce heat to 350°F and bake another 20 minutes until nicely browned. Serve immediately.

Serves 4-6

ASPARAGUS SOUFFLÉ

Serve this as a first course for dinner or at the center of a lunch and you'll discover an excellent way to bring the flavor of spring to the table.

2 pounds asparagus, peeled and cooked
2 potatoes, cooked, peeled and cubed
½ cup ricotta
¼ teaspoon red pepper flakes
2 tablespoons scallions, minced
Salt and pepper
8 eggs, separated

1. Drain asparagus and potatoes thoroughly. Puree briefly in processor with ricotta. Add red pepper flakes, scallions and salt and pepper to taste.
2. Transfer asparagus-potato mixture to a large bowl. Whip egg yolks and then blend well with vegetable mixture.
3. Beat egg whites in separate bowl until they form soft peaks. Fold one-fourth of the egg whites carefully into the asparagus mixture. Then fold remainder of egg whites into the mixture, being careful not to overmix.
4. Correct seasonings, then immediately scoop mixture into well-buttered, chilled soufflé dish or dishes, place dish on baking sheet and bake at 425°F for about 15 minutes.

Serves 6-8

ASPARAGUS FLAN

Easier than a soufflé, this versatile dish can be a first course or part of a main course. As a first course, nap it with asparagus sauce (see page 20). As a main dish, pair it with, say, salmon or chicken breasts, using whatever sauce is appropriate for the salmon or chicken on the flan, also.

> 2 dozen asparagus spears, peeled and
>   cooked
> 2 eggs
> 2 egg yolks
>   Salt and pepper
> ⅔ cup milk
> ⅔ cup cream
>   Dash Tabasco

1. Cut off and reserve 8 asparagus tips. Cut remaining asparagus into pieces and puree in processor, blender or food mill. Measure 1 cup puree and reserve remainder for another use.
2. Combine puree, eggs and yolks. Salt and pepper to taste. Heat milk and cream to nearly boiling and combine with asparagus mixture. Add dash of Tabasco and stir.
3. Butter 8 flan molds. Fill with mixture. Place molds in baking pan and pour boiling water into pan to halfway up sides of molds. Bake at 325°F for about 25 minutes, until tip of knife inserted in flan comes out clean. Unmold, top each with reserved asparagus tip and serve immediately.

Serves 8

ASPARAGUS PUDDING

Whole asparagus spears make this a substantial dish that could serve as a main course for lunch or as a light supper.

> 2½ cups asparagus, peeled and barely
>   cooked, in ½-inch pieces
> 10 tablespoons butter
>   Salt and pepper
> ½ cup flour
> 2 cups milk, scalded with ½ cup cream
> 4 egg yolks
> 3 tablespoons grated Parmesan
> 2 tablespoons bread crumbs

1. Sauté asparagus pieces in 2 tablespoons of the butter 8-10 minutes, until quite tender. Salt and pepper to taste and cool.
2. Prepare béchamel by melting remaining butter in small pan over low heat. When it stops foaming, beat in flour and cook, stirring, 2 minutes without allowing to color. Remove from heat and pour in scalded milk and cream all at once, beating to blend. Return pan to medium-high heat and, stirring, bring to boil..Boil 2-3 minutes, stirring constantly. Salt to taste. Let cool.
3. When béchamel is cooled, beat in egg yolks and Parmesan. Mix in asparagus.
4. Butter a 1½- or 2-quart baking dish and sprinkle with bread crumbs. Pour in asparagus mixture. Place dish in baking pan and pour in boiling water to halfway up sides of dish. Bake at 400°F for about 75 minutes, covering dish with foil after 1 hour. Pudding is done when wood pick inserted in middle comes out clean. Serve hot.

Serves 6-8

ASPARAGUS MILANESE

An excellent brunch dish, this classic Italian preparation also can serve as a first course for dinner.

> 2 pounds asparagus, barely cooked
> 8 tablespoons butter
> ½ cup grated Parmesan cheese
> 4 eggs
> Salt and pepper

1. Sauté cooked asparagus gently in 4 tablespoons of the butter for about 4 minutes, until heated through. Remove to hot serving platter, sectioning into four servings. Sprinkle with Parmesan and keep warm.
2. Fry eggs sunny-side up in the remaining 4 tablespoons butter. Place an egg on each portion of asparagus, douse with butter from the skillet, salt and pepper to taste and serve hot.

Serves 4

ASPARAGUS CREPES

This is a way of moving asparagus to the center of a meal, either as a lunch or light supper. It also works as a first course for a more elaborate dinner.

> 1½ pounds asparagus, peeled and cooked
> ½ cup grated Parmesan
> ¾ cup goat cheese, crumbled

Crepe Batter

> 4 eggs
> 1 cup milk
> 1¼ cups flour
> ¼ cup water
> ½ teaspoon salt
> 3 tablespoons melted butter, cooled

Bechamel

> 4 tablespoons butter
> 4 tablespoons flour
> 2 cups milk, scalded
> Salt

For Frying

> 3 tablespoons melted butter
> 1 tablespoon oil

1. Mash asparagus through sieve (to yield at least 1 cup).
2. To prepare crepes, mix all ingredients except butter in processor or blender. Stir in butter. Thin batter with milk, if necessary, to consistency of heavy cream. Brush 7-inch skillet with some of the melted butter-oil mixture and place on medium-high heat. When skillet is hot, add about 3 tablespoons batter and swirl quickly to coat skillet. Cook until light gold, about 1 minute, flip and cook 30 seconds more. Cool on rack. (Stack between sheets of waxed paper and cover with plastic wrap if not using immediately.)
3. Prepare béchamel by melting butter in small pan over low heat. When it stops foaming, beat in flour and cook, stirring, 2 minutes without allowing to color. Remove from heat and pour in scalded milk all at once, beating to blend. Return pan to medium-high heat and, stirring, bring to boil. Boil 2-3 minutes, stirring mixture constantly. Salt to taste.
4. Remove from heat and stir in ¼ cup of the Parmesan to dissolve. Mix ½ cup béchamel with mashed asparagus.
5. To assemble, spread 2 tablespoons of the asparagus mixture onto each crepe, leaving a ½-inch border around edge. Sprinkle about 1 tablespoon goat cheese on each crepe. Fold each crepe into quarters.
6. Slightly overlap crepes in shallow, well-buttered baking dish. Mask with béchamel. Sprinkle with remaining ¼ cup Parmesan. Bake at 375°F for 15-20 minutes, until heated through, then place crepes under broiler for 1 minute or so to brown lightly. Serve immediately.

Makes 12 crepes

Asparagus Milanese

Asparagus Crepes

ASPARAGUS SAUCE

A versatile sauce, this can be served hot over hot asparagus, cold with cold asparagus, or at room temperature over cold hard-boiled eggs. It also makes an excellent hot or cold sauce for hot or cold poached white fish. In the latter case, it benefits from doubling the amount of cream and adding some fresh dill when the sauce is pureed.

> 12 stalks peeled, cooked asparagus
> 4 scallions, chopped
> 2 tablespoons butter
>   Pinch of sugar
>   Salt and pepper
> 2 tablespoons cream
>   Lemon juice

1. Sauté asparagus and scallions in butter for 5-8 minutes, until quite tender. Season mixture with sugar, salt and pepper to taste.
2. Puree in blender or processor. Reheat in saucepan over medium-low heat, then whisk in cream and a few drops of lemon juice.

Serves 4-6

ASPARAGUS FRITTERS

Quick and easy, these fritters accompany any meat or fish.

> 2 cups 1-inch pieces asparagus, peeled and cooked
> ½ cup minced onion
> 4 tablespoons butter
> ½ pound button mushrooms, chopped finely
> 1 cup fresh bread crumbs
> ¾ cup grated Parmesan
> 6 eggs
> 2 tablespoons olive oil
> 6 basil leaves, chopped (or 1 teaspoon dried)
>   Salt and pepper
>   Dash Tabasco

1. Puree asparagus in processor, blender or food mill.
2. Sauté onion in half the butter 10 minutes over low heat. Sauté mushrooms in remaining butter until their liquid has evaporated, about 10 minutes.
3. Combine all ingredients. Heat ¼-inch vegetable oil in skillet until light haze forms over top. Form fritters by dropping heaping tablespoons of mixture into hot oil and pressing fritters down with a fork to about ¼-inch thickness. Cook until brown, then flip and brown the other side. Serve hot with fresh lemon wedges.

Serves 6-10

CREAM OF ASPARAGUS SOUP

Asparagus soup is served cold or hot. This is a simple version featuring intense asparagus flavor.

> 1½ pounds asparagus
> 2 cups chopped onion
> 4 tablespoons butter
> 4 cups chicken stock
> ¼ cup minced parsley
> ½ cup cream
>   Salt and white pepper

1. Cut tips off the asparagus and reserve. Snap off the woody butt-ends of asparagus and discard. Cut the stalks into ½-inch pieces.
2. Sauté onion in butter over low heat in heavy pot for about 20 minutes, until transparent. Add chicken stock and bring to boil. Add asparagus stalks, cover, reduce heat and simmer 45 minutes.
3. In blender or processor, puree asparagus in stock along with parsley. Press puree through medium sieve.
4. Return soup to pot, add asparagus tips and simmer until tips are tender, 5-8 minutes.
5. Stir in cream, salt and pepper to taste and serve.

Serves 4

PORK WITH ASPARAGUS

Andy Ma, estimable chef at Andy and Jemmy's Wok in Seattle, says this Mandarin-style dish is his favorite method of preparing asparagus.

> 1 pound lean pork loin, sliced thinly
> 2 eggs
> 2 tablespoons cornstarch
> 2 pounds asparagus
>   Vegetable oil
> ½ cup chicken broth
>   Salt
> 1 tablespoon sesame oil

1. Soak pork in salted water for 2 hours, drain and dry thoroughly. Beat eggs with 1 tablespoon cornstarch, mix with pork and marinate in the refrigerator 24 hours.
2. Break off woody ends of asparagus and peel stalks if tough. Cut asparagus on the bias into 3-inch lengths.
3. Swirl vegetable oil in hot wok to coat cooking area. Sear pork over high heat for about 30 seconds. Add chicken broth, asparagus and salt to taste. Stir frequently and cook fast so that asparagus remains crisp.
4. Just before serving, swirl in remaining tablespoon cornstarch and the sesame oil. Serve immediately.

Serves 4

ASPARAGUS SAUCE FOR PASTA

"Primavera" means springtime in Italian. Here's a pasta sauce truly deserving of that overused term.

> 1½ pounds asparagus, peeled
> ½ pound thick-sliced bacon, in ½-inch cross-slices
> 1 cup dry vermouth
> 2½ cups cream
>   Salt and pepper
>   Pinch red pepper flakes
> ½ cup grated Parmesan
> 1 pound linguine

1. Cut asparagus in 2-inch pieces. Boil in salted water until barely cooked, about 6 minutes. Drain, plunge immediately in cold water and drain again.
2. Sauté bacon in heavy saucepan until crisp. Remove and reserve. Pour off all but 2 tablespoons of the fat. Add vermouth and boil to reduce by half. Add cream, salt and pepper to taste, and red pepper flakes. Bring to boil, reduce heat and simmer until reduced by one-third.
3. Reduce heat to warm, stir in Parmesan, and add asparagus and bacon.
4. Meanwhile, cook linguine in boiling salted water. Drain and place in warm bowl. Toss gently with sauce and serve immediately.

Serves 4-6

ASPARAGUS FRITTATA

Here's another way to enjoy the affinity of asparagus and eggs, using the Italian omelet method.

> 1 pound asparagus, peeled and barely cooked
> 6 eggs
> 2 tablespoons water
>   Salt and pepper
> ⅔ cup grated Parmesan
> ¼ cup minced parsley
> 4 tablespoons butter

1. Plunge asparagus into cold water after cooking, to retain color. Drain and cut into ½-inch pieces.
2. Beat eggs with water. Salt and pepper to taste. Stir in asparagus, Parmesan and parsley.
3. Melt butter in heavy skillet over low heat. Pour in asparagus-egg mixture and cook 12-15 minutes until eggs are set and only top is runny. Place under broiler about 1 minute, just to set top. Serve warm or cold.

Serves 4

21

SAUCES FOR ASPARAGUS

Freshly cooked asparagus is enhanced by any number of sauces. Here are a few suggestions from various cuisines: Maltaise, an orange-flavored Hollandaise from France; Salsa Verde with walnuts, from Italy; an Oriental blend; and a Mediterranean mayonnaise.

Sauce Maltaise

> 2 tablespoons white wine vinegar
> 1 tablespoon water
>   Pinch salt
> 3 egg yolks
> ½ pound butter, melted and cooled slightly
> 3 tablespoons orange juice
> 1 tablespoon orange zest
>   White pepper

1. Boil vinegar, water and salt until reduced by one-half. Let cool slightly. Beat in egg yolks over extremely gentle heat (or barely simmering water) until sauce is thick and creamy, 1-2 minutes.
2. Remove from heat and beat in lukewarm butter a few drops at a time at first and then more rapidly until sauce becomes quite thick. (Do not use milky residue at bottom of pan.)
3. Beat in orange juice little by little and then stir in orange zest. Season with pepper and more salt to taste. Serve warm, not hot, with warm asparagus.

Note: *Depending on size of egg yolks, you might not be able to use all the butter and keep the sauce together. Also, in first stage, as you beat egg yolks, make certain they don't thicken too quickly or become lumpy. Remove from heat if that begins to happen and plunge bottom of pan into cold water.*

Salsa Verde with Walnuts

> 1 bunch parsley
> 4-5 basil leaves
> 2-3 mint leaves (optional)
>   Handful watercress (optional)
> 2 cloves garlic
> 4 ounces shelled walnuts, finely chopped
>   Salt and pepper
> 2 hard-boiled egg yolks, chopped
> 1 cup olive oil

1. Chop parsley, basil, mint, watercress and garlic together until very fine. (Or process together quickly.)
2. Mix with walnuts. Add salt and pepper to taste.
3. Mix in egg yolks, then olive oil slowly until sauce is smooth. Chill before serving with cold asparagus.

Oriental Sauce

> 2 tablespoons light soy sauce
> 1 tablespoon sesame oil
> 1 tablespoon sugar
> 1 tablespoon red wine vinegar
> 1 tablespoon sherry
> 1 clove garlic, minced

Mix all ingredients. Serve with warm or room-temperature asparagus.

Garlic Mayonnaise

> 3 cloves garlic, minced
> 1 egg
> 1 tablespoon lemon juice
> 1 teaspoon salt
> 1 teaspoon pepper
> 1 cup olive oil

1. Combine all ingredients except oil in processor or blender and process or blend 2 minutes. Slowly add oil as machine runs.
2. Adjust salt, pepper and lemon juice to taste. Serve with cold asparagus.

BERRIES

"Doubtless God could have made a better berry, but doubtless God never did," an Englishman once said of the strawberry. Clearly he hadn't visited Washington. If he had, he could not have been quite so certain of divine preference.

Here he would have encountered a veritable Eden of berries west of the Cascade Mountains, where climate and soil create a haven for these fruits. He would have found his beloved strawberry, to be sure. But he also would have discovered red raspberries, black raspberries, blackberries, blueberries, cranberries, gooseberries and currants, to name only the cultivated choices. And, with a little effort, he could have sampled Oregon grape, buffalo berries, huckleberries, salal berries, bearberries, silverberries, serviceberries and rose hips, to mention some of the native berries favored by coastal Indians. After eating his way through a Washington summer, would this Englishman, stained of mouth and lips, have been so glib?

Or would he have understood the Master's plan, the savory journey from June to November that leads from strawberry, to raspberry, to blueberry, to blackberry, to cranberry—and makes unnecessary the silliness of choosing perfection over perfection?

Washington cooks comprehend this

sweet progression. Many also know, as did the Indians before them, that there is more to berry season than eating. There is picking, too, a merry chore in the company of others. Indian women and girls were said to have gone off on berry expeditions with great gaiety. Not only were they supplementing their diets with much-needed vitamins, they also were getting away from their villages and the company of men.

Berries played an important role in the Americas long before white men arrived. Indians bearing wicker baskets of dried blueberries greeted the Pilgrims, testimony not only to the Indians' hospitality but to the value they assigned to berries. Lewis and Clark shared meals with Indians of smoke-cured venison into which dried berries had been pounded.

In Washington, as in no other state, the full range of America's berries remains important. Of the significant commercial berry crops in the nation, Washington ranks among the top five producing states for each: first in red raspberries, second in black raspberries and blackberries, fourth in cranberries and blueberries, and fifth in strawberries.

For Washington cooks, this means local berries are readily available in markets, on roadside stands and in U-pick fields throughout the summer. U-pick operations have become popular because

BLUEBERRY-RASPBERRY TART

A beautiful mosaic, this tart combines two berries whose seasons luckily overlap. Failing a supply of either, make it with just one type of berry, or substitute others.

    8 ounces cream cheese
    1/3 cup sugar
    1/2 cup crème fraiche (see Notes on
        Ingredients, page xi)
    2 eggs
    1 teaspoon lemon juice
      Pinch cinnamon
    1 9-inch tart shell (see below)
    1 pint raspberries
    1/2 pint blueberries
      Red currant jelly, melted

1. Blend cream cheese and sugar in processor or blender until smooth. Add crème fraiche and blend for a few seconds. With machine running, add eggs one at a time. Then add the lemon juice and cinnamon.
2. Pour filling into cooled tart shell. Arrange one row of blueberries in single layer around edge of shell. Fill center with single layer of raspberries. Bake at 350°F for 25 minutes, or until wood pick inserted in center comes out clean. Cool on rack. Gently brush with melted red currant jelly. Remove pan rim. Serve with whipped cream.

Serves 6-8

Tart Shell

    1 1/2 cups flour
    1 1/2 tablespoons sugar
        Pinch salt
      2 teaspoons lemon juice
      1 egg yolk
     10 tablespoons unsalted butter,
        chilled and cut into bits
    2-3 tablespoons ice water

1. Combine flour, sugar and salt in processor and process until mixed. Add lemon juice and egg yolk and process to blend. Add butter and process until mixture breaks into pea-size bits. Add ice water a little at a time until dough masses around blade.
2. Remove dough from processor and form into ball. Cover with plastic wrap and chill until firm, about 30 minutes. (Dough may be frozen and brought to room temperature before rolling out.)
3. For above recipe, roll out dough to cover 9-inch tart pan with removable rim. Press dough into flutes on rim and trim along rim top.
4. Prick shell all over with fork. Line shell with waxed paper and fill paper with dried beans or rice. Bake at 350°F for 15 minutes. Remove beans or rice and waxed paper. Bake about 15 minutes more, until shell is pale gold. Cool on rack. Brush with syrup made by dissolving 3 tablespoons sugar in 2 tablespoons water and boiling 5 minutes, brushing crystals from sides of pan as syrup cooks.
5. Return shell to hot oven 5 minutes to set.

Gregg Greene picking berries at Carnation.

they make financial sense and afford consumers the opportunity of gathering fruit in prime condition and partaking of the singular pleasure of berry picking.

Picking one's own berries also means being able to taste them at their peak, whether damp with cool morning dew or warmed by the afternoon sun. Failing that, consumers should seek berries that are plump, dry and of full color. Blueberries are an exception to the latter rule; they are usually best when they have a light powdery-blue color.

Here's a look at Washington's berries, crop by crop:

Strawberries—Strawberries grow wild in many parts of the world. The cultivated strawberry's origins, however, are in the New World. Here, in Virginia, there was a small, scarlet strawberry and, on the west coast of South America, a large, pale strawberry. In the mid-18th century, French botanists brought them together, a marriage resulting in the dozens of varieties we know today.

Unhappily, the same science that

DOUBLE BLUEBERRY PIE

Raw and cooked blueberries blend in this pie to create a dessert brimming with the essence of the berries.

> *4 cups blueberries*
> *¾ cup sugar*
> *3 tablespoons cornstarch*
> *1 tablespoon lemon juice*
> *½ teaspoon lemon zest*
> *1 tablespoon butter*
> *1 9-inch pie shell, baked*
> *½ cup heavy cream*
> *2 tablespoons sugar*

1. Combine 2 cups of the berries, ¾ cup sugar and cornstarch in double boiler over medium-high heat and cook 10-12 minutes, until very thick, stirring frequently.
2. Remove from heat and stir in lemon juice, zest and butter. Spread half the mixture on bottom and sides of pie shell. Spread uncooked berries over cooked mixture, then cover with remainder of mixture.
3. Whip cream with 2 tablespoons sugar and spread over top. Chill.

Serves 6-8

BLUEBERRY PUDDING

A simple but elegant dish, this "pudding" marries the crunch of sweet croutons and the softness of warm berries.

> *1 quart blueberries*
> *2 tablespoons sugar*
> *½ teaspoon cinnamon*
> *1 cup cream*
> *4 slices stale white bread*
> *8 tablespoons butter*
> *⅔ cup sugar*

1. Wash and pick over berries. Drain.
2. Mix 2 tablespoons sugar and cinnamon. Whip cream until stiff but not dry and fold in sugar-cinnamon mixture. Refrigerate.
3. Remove crusts from bread and cut into cubes. Melt butter in skillet over medium heat until frothy. Sauté croutons until crisp. Add ⅔ cup sugar and stir to coat croutons.
4. Just before serving, reheat croutons, add berries and warm through. Serve immediately with the whipped cream.

Serves 6-8

BLUEBERRY-APPLE CRISP

This old standby is updated here with the addition of pecans to the topping and a blend of tart apples and sweet blueberries.

> *2 cups blueberries*
> *2 apples, peeled, cored and sliced thinly*
> *2 teaspoons lemon juice*
> *1 teaspoon lemon zest*
> *¾ cup brown sugar*

Topping

> *1¼ cups flour*
> *½ cup sugar*
> *1 teaspoon baking powder*
> *½ teaspoon salt*
> *6 tablespoons butter*
> *1 egg, beaten*
> *1 cup shelled pecans, chopped coarsely*
> *½ teaspoon cinnamon*

1. Mix fruit, lemon juice and zest, and sugar, and spread in large pie plate.
2. For the topping, mix flour, sugar, baking powder and salt. Cut in butter, then mix in egg, pecans and cinnamon. Spread evenly over fruit. Bake at 400°F for 30 minutes. Serve with cream or ice cream.

Serves 8

Double
Blueberry
Pie

Blueberry
Pudding

Blueberry-
Apple Crisp

created great-tasting strawberries now is employed in the destruction of that ineffable flavor. Growers favor varieties that can be easily picked, withstand journeys to far markets and look red—and big—in the store. In breeding for such berries, something has to give. That something is taste. As one Washington berry authority says ruefully, "Taste is not a criterion that motivates people buying strawberries these days. Most people don't know what a strawberry should taste like anyway because they have never had a chance to taste a real one." The huge California berries available in Washington during the winter and early spring, for instance, often can't be distinguished by taste from their cardboard containers.

Happily, Washington's strawberries are designed to be sold closer to home and therefore taste better. Washington's sunny days and cool nights during the early summer also are especially good for developing strawberry flavor.

Like all soft berries, strawberries shouldn't be washed or hulled until just before they're used. If you refrigerate strawberries, cover them tightly or their aroma will take over the refrigerator.

Raspberries—A couple of weeks after Washington strawberries ripen, usually in late June, raspberries arrive. Raspberries, like blackberries, share the same family tree as the rose. Raspberries are distinguished from blackberries by their cores. When picked, a raspberry separates from its core, or "receptacle," while a blackberry's core is part of the fruit.

Many people consider raspberries to be ideal only when eaten raw—as long as the berries' tartness is balanced by sugar and they're dressed with cream. Raspberries require especially delicate treatment. They must be kept cool but not cold since they quickly lose aroma and flavor if chilled. They're also vulnerable to mildew. If they are to be eaten with sugar, sprinkle it on right away to help preserve them. Rinse raspberries if you wish—but quickly, by dropping a few at a time into a pan of cold water. Raspberries grow high off the ground; if handled properly, they can be eaten without washing.

Blueberries—

Blueberries as big as the end of your thumb,
Real sky-blue, and heavy, and ready to drum
In the cavernous pail of the first one to come!

Thus did Robert Frost describe the blueberry picker's eager anticipation. Had he been a Washingtonian instead of a New Englander, Frost might also have written of the breathtaking beauty of wild Western blueberry bushes encountered on an autumn hike.

Washington grows blueberries that excel in taste and appearance. Unlike crops from Michigan and New Jersey, the two largest-producing states, Washington's blueberries have to appeal to the fresh-market consumer because fully a third of Washington's crop reaches that market rather than being processed. As a result, Washington berries tend to be sweeter, have fuller flavor and look better than their eastern cousins.

Wild blueberries often are confused with huckleberries. Seeds distinguish them: huckleberries have 10 large, hard seeds; blueberries have many tiny, soft seeds. Huckleberries do grow in Washington, however, relatives of what is said to be the oldest living thing on Earth: a 13,000-year-old huckleberry vine covering hundreds of acres in western Pennsylvania.

Blackberries—In "Song of Myself," Whitman said, "The running blackberry would adorn the parlors of heaven," proving that not only Englishmen can wax poetic about their favorite berry. Whitman was writing of the wild blackberry, the so-called "trailer" or "dewberry." Wild varieties can be found in Washington, though they are increasingly rare. Wild blackberries have intense flavor and are worth the effort—and scratches—to gather.

Most "wild" blackberries in Washington, however, are simply hybrids that have taken over roadsides and woods. Cultivated blackberries, all hybrids, have many names: Young, Logan, Boysen, Cascade, Olympic and Marion, to cite the most

BLUEBERRY CHUTNEY

Here's a chutney that helps carry the summer flavor of blueberries into winter, if it's preserved. Otherwise, leave it in the refrigerator for a day or so and serve with meat, fish and even sandwiches.

5 cups cider vinegar
2½ cups sugar
2 teaspoons ground ginger
2 teaspoons dry mustard
1 teaspoon cayenne (or to taste)
4 sticks cinnamon
½ teaspoon ground cinnamon
1 cup raisins
2 cups candied papaya, cut into small pieces
2 tablespoons whole cloves
2 tablespoons salt
4 pints blueberries
Zest of 2 lemons
Zest of 2 oranges
2 cups slivered almonds

1. In a large, noncorrosive pan, combine 4 cups of the vinegar with the sugar. Boil until syrupy, about 20 minutes, reducing to about 4 cups.
2. Add remaining vinegar, ginger, mustard, cayenne, cinnamon sticks and cinnamon, raisins, papaya, cloves and salt. Bring to boil, reduce heat and simmer 10 minutes.
3. Turn heat up to high, bring to boil and add blueberries, lemon and orange zest and almonds. Stir, submerging the berries, and cook just until berries begin to pop.
4. Cool and refrigerate or preserve according to your normal canning procedure.

Makes about 5 pints

BLUEBERRY SAUCE FOR MEAT

Surprisingly, blueberries make an excellent sauce for some meats such as duck, game hens and pork. Though the sweetness of fruit sauces is not to everyone's taste, this one is nicely balanced. Any red wine vinegar works with this sauce, but the non-sourness of the balsamic vinegar called for here is ideal.

1 cup blueberries
⅔ cup white wine
⅔ cup strong chicken stock
Sugar
½ cup balsamic vinegar
⅓ cup fresh mint, minced
2 tablespoons crème de cassis
¼ cup unsalted butter
Salt and pepper
Lemon juice

1. Simmer blueberries with wine, stock and 1 tablespoon sugar for 5 minutes. Process until smooth. Strain.
2. Boil vinegar and 2 teaspoons sugar in a small pan for 5 minutes or until about 2 tablespoons of syrup remain. Add to sauce along with mint and crème de cassis.
3. Add defatted juices, if any, from broiled, roasted or sautéed meat to sauce. Reheat gently and whisk in butter. Salt and pepper to taste and add lemon juice to taste if desired. Serve immediately.

prominent. Many of these are popularly thought to be crosses between blackberries and raspberries, but only one, the Tayberry, which is gaining favor in Washington, is a true raspberry-blackberry cross. (Developed in Scotland, it's named for that country's River Tay.)

Currants and Gooseberries—Closely related, currants and gooseberries are not nearly as popular in the US as they are in Europe, so very few are grown anywhere in this country.

About 40 years ago, little Vashon Island in Puget Sound was the currant capital of America, with several hundred acres in plantings. The market didn't support such production, however, and most of Vashon's currants were abandoned. Now, small-scale Vashon growers, along with growers near Prosser in Eastern Washington, are reviving currants in Washington.

Few currants reach the fresh market; most go into red currant jelly. Some home gardeners, however, sell red currants at roadside stands and in farmers' markets during the July harvest.

Black currants, a separate species, nearly disappeared from the US because they are host to a white pine disease called "blister rust" and were under quarantine in many states. The quarantine has been lifted in Washington; native wild currants could not be eradicated and the native white pine was dying off anyway. Black currants are making a tentative comeback, which is good news for cooks. Black currants have a wilder, stronger flavor than red currants, just right for game. (Black currants are the basis of crème de cassis.)

Gooseberries are nearly as hard to find as currants, though, again, some do reach the fresh market. Gooseberries come in several colors: red, green, pink, and white.

Few people can tolerate them raw since gooseberries are quite tart and their skins are tough. Unless you intend to strain them into a puree, gooseberries must be "topped and tailed," or pared of their stem and blossom ends. Look for them alongside currants in July.

Cranberries—Though there are several species of wild cranberries in the world, including one in Washington, only the large cranberry native to the US East Coast has been widely cultivated. Cranberries were in important part of the East Coast Indians' diet. Early settlers found them too tart to eat until the Indians taught them to sweeten the berries with maple syrup.

The cultivated cranberry came west to Washington in 1883, when a French-Canadian settler established a bog of Cape Cod cranberries on Long Beach Peninsula, just north of the Columbia River. Over the next 30 years, other bogs were established in that area as well as the Grayland region of Pacific and Grays Harbor counties.

Cranberries flourish on the Washington coast, where conditions are similar to the cranberry areas of the Northeast. The Washington harvest begins in late September and runs until about Thanksgiving, when Americans pay special attention to cranberries. Cranberries, however, freeze well and can be eaten year-round. Before using them, be sure to pick out under- or over-ripe fruit.

STRAWBERRIES FLAMBÉ
(Ice cream topping)

This is a simple way to vary your strawberry offerings. Adjust the proportions to taste.

> 4 tablespoons sugar
> 4 tablespoons water
> 4 tablespoons orange marmalade
> 1 quart strawberries
> ½ cup brandy

1. Cook sugar and water in skillet over medium heat, stirring, until sugar dissolves. Add marmalade and stir. Add hulled berries, warm through and spoon into serving dish.
2. Warm brandy in small pan, ignite, pour over berries and serve immediately over ice cream.

Serves 6-8

STRAWBERRY-CHEESE TORTE

Jan Weaver of The Wedge, a Seattle delicatessen, frequently prepares this simple combination of cheeses and berries for parties. Although the recipe specifies Brie, she also uses Camembert, which comes in smaller rounds, for small parties. If mascarpone is not available, use cream cheese. But the cream cheese must be fresh and not contain vegetable gum.

> 3-4 pints strawberries, hulled
> 2 pounds mascarpone
> 1-kilogram round of Brie

1. Lightly crush, but do not puree, berries. Mix with mascarpone.
2. Slice Brie horizontally into two discs. Spread a layer of the strawberry-cheese mixture on the bottom disc, cover with top disc and cover outside with strawberry-cheese mixture as you would frost a cake.

Serves about 16

STRAWBERRY SHORTCAKE

Many are the recipes for this American standard. This one is special, however. It's said to have been the late James Beard's favorite. Serve it with any berry, or even, say, peaches.

> 3-4 pints strawberries, hulled, sliced and sweetened to taste
> 4 cups flour
> ¼ cup plus 2 tablespoons sugar
> 3½ teaspoons cream of tartar
> 1¾ teaspoons baking soda
> 2 teaspoons salt
> 12 tablespoons unsalted butter, chilled and cut into bits
> 1½ cups cream
> 4 hard-boiled egg yolks, mashed
> 4 tablespoons unsalted butter, melted

1. Sift flour with ¼ cup plus 2 tablespoons of the sugar, cream of tartar, baking soda and salt. Cut in chilled butter with knives or pastry cutter. Stir in cream and egg yolks quickly until shaggy dough forms.
2. Knead dough on floured surface a few times, pat out to ¾-inch thickness. Cut out 6-8 rounds 3 inches in diameter with cookie cutter or sharp-edged glass. Cut out equal number of 2½-inch rounds.
3. Place larger rounds on oiled baking sheet, brush with melted butter, top with smaller rounds and brush those with melted butter.
4. Bake at 375°F for 15-18 minutes, until cakes are firm and brown.
5. Remove tops from cakes, spoon sliced and sweetened berries over bottoms, replace tops and spoon more berries over. Serve with slightly sweetened whipped cream.

Serves 6-8

Strawberries
Flambé

Strawberry-
Cheese
Torte

Strawberry
Shortcake

STRAWBERRY-ALMOND BUTTER

This spread is intended for toast, pancakes, waffles, biscuits, scones or just about anything warm.

½ pound butter, softened
1 cup superfine sugar
1 pound strawberries, hulled
1 cup ground almonds
¼ teaspoon salt

1. Process butter with sugar until creamy and sugar crystals have disappeared. Remove to bowl.
2. Process berries 10-15 seconds, but do not liquefy. Return butter-sugar mixture to processor bowl with almonds and salt, and process until mixture is blended.

STRAWBERRY SOUFFLÉ WITH RASPBERRY SAUCE

This recipe exploits the juxtaposition of strawberry and raspberry seasons.

4 eggs, separated
¾ cup sugar
2 tablespoons lemon juice
2 pints strawberries, hulled
2 tablespoons Cointreau
1 tablespoon unflavored gelatin
2 tablespoons cold water
1½ cups cream

1. Beat egg yolks with sugar until light-colored and thickened. Beat in lemon juice. Puree strawberries in processor or blender until smooth but not liquid. Stir in Cointreau.

2. Soften gelatin in the cold water. Dissolve by placing container holding gelatin in pan of simmering water. Simmer, stirring, until dissolved.
3. Combine strawberry puree and egg-sugar mixture. Stirring, add dissolved gelatin in a slow stream to the strawberry mixture.
4. Whip cream. Clean beaters and whip egg whites until stiff but not dry.
5. Fold whipped cream into strawberry mixture. Fold in egg whites. Scrape into soufflé dish and chill in refrigerator until set. Serve chilled with raspberry sauce.

Serves 6-8

Raspberry Sauce

2 pints raspberries
1 cup superfine sugar (or to taste)
2 tablespoons Cointreau

Puree berries in a processor or blender. Strain. Stir in the sugar and Cointreau. Serve.

COLD RASPBERRY SOUP

Though the Russians and Scandinavians would disagree, not everyone finds berry soups to his liking. This soup, however, can be surprisingly refreshing on a hot day. Strawberries may be substituted, but the amount of sugar should be reduced.

2 cups raspberries
⅓ to ½ cup sugar
½ cup sour cream
2 cups cold water
½ cup red wine
Fresh mint leaves

1. Rub berries through fine sieve or process in food mill, setting aside a few berries for garnish.
2. Mix berries and sugar to taste. Add sour cream, water and wine.
3. Heat slowly in heavy saucepan, stirring constantly. Do not boil.
4. Chill. Serve with mint leaves and whole berries as garnish.

Serves 4-6

SUMMER PUDDING

Devised in England a century ago for hospital patients who had to avoid rich desserts, summer pudding is a delightful way to exploit the overlapping berry seasons. Proportions below are not exact since they depend on the size of the mold.

About 3 quarts mixed berries
  (strawberries, raspberries, blueberries,
  red currants, blackberries, etc.)
Sugar
1 loaf firm white bread, slightly stale,
  sliced
Whipped cream

1. Mix berries with sugar to taste. Simmer 2-3 minutes until sugar melts and juices run.
2. Select straight-sided, round baking pan, soufflé dish or charlotte mold. Line with plastic wrap, leaving an ample overhang.
3. Remove crusts from bread slices. To cover bottom with bread, lay out 4 slices in a square, place pan on them and cut around to yield 4 wedges that fit snugly into bottom of pan. Repeat twice to get wedges that will fit on top and as a layer in middle.
4. Trim other bread slices to fit exactly, standing up, around inside of pan.
5. Line bottom of pan with 4 wedges of bread. Pour half of berries and juice into pan, place the bread layer on top and pour remaining berries and juice on that. Top with remaining wedges. Fold over overhanging plastic wrap.
6. Fit inverted plate into top of pan and press down hard. Place heavy weight on plate and refrigerate 6-8 hours. To unmold, loosen pudding by pulling gently on plastic wrap, spread out plastic wrap, place plate on top of mold and invert. Remove the plastic wrap and serve with sweetened whipped cream.

Serves 6-8

HAZELNUT MERINGUE WITH RASPBERRIES

Nearly any soft fruit—strawberries, for instance, or blueberries or peaches—can be used in this recipe. But none surpasses tart fresh raspberries as a foil for the sweet, chewy meringue. Though this dessert has high style, it's quite easily prepared.

¾ cup shelled hazelnuts
5 egg whites
1¼ cups sugar
½ teaspoon white wine vinegar
1¼ cups cream
2 cups raspberries

1. Spread nuts in a single layer on a baking pan and toast in 300°F oven for 10 minutes. Cool, then powder in a processor or nut mill.
2. Beat egg whites until almost stiff then beat in sugar a little at a time, finally beating in vinegar. Fold in nuts.
3. Using one or more baking sheets lined with cooking parchment, spread the meringue in ¼-inch-deep rounds 3 inches in diameter, smoothing tops. There should be enough for 16 rounds. (Or make two rounds of about 10 inches each, if a single dessert rather than individual ones is desired.)
4. Bake meringue at 350°F for about 30 minutes, watching that it doesn't overbrown. Cool.
5. Just before serving, whip cream, adding sugar to taste, and fold in 1 cup of fruit. Spread mixture on meringue round, dot with remaining whole fruit and serve open-faced, or top with second meringue round.

Serves 8

**Raspberries
and Toasted
Oats**

**Cranberry
Sherbet**

**Cranberry-
Cornbread
Stuffing**

RASPBERRIES AND TOASTED OATS

From Scotland comes this simple dessert combining several of the Scots' favorite foods. (Blackberries substitute nicely for the raspberries.)

1 cup rolled oats
1 cup cream
1 tablespoon sugar
2 teaspoons Scotch or brandy
1 pint raspberries

1. Toast oats on ungreased baking sheet in 400°F oven 10-12 minutes, shaking sheet occasionally. Cool.
2. Whip cream with sugar. Stir in Scotch or brandy. Fold in toasted oats.
3. Beginning with cream, layer cream and berries into dessert glasses, making sure to end with a layer of berries. Serve immediately.

Serves 4

CRANBERRY SHERBET

Either as a dessert or as an accompaniment to roast pork or fowl, this recipe brings the flavor of cranberries to the table in a new form.

2 cups cranberries
1½ cups water
1 teaspoon unflavored gelatin soaked in 2 tablespoons water
3 tablespoons lemon juice
1¼ cups sugar
1 cup orange juice
2 egg whites, beaten stiff

1. Cook cranberries in water until tender, 10-12 minutes. Mash through food mill. Add soaked gelatin, lemon juice, sugar and orange juice. Mix well. Pour into pan. Place in freezer.
2. When partially frozen, beat well with egg beater and fold in egg whites. Return to freezer until frozen.

Serves 6-8

CRANBERRY-CORNBREAD STUFFING

This goes well with any fowl, or on its own. If you don't have a bird, bake the stuffing 40-45 minutes at 325°F in a covered casserole, adding 1 cup poultry stock to the basic recipe.

3 cups cranberries
2 cups chopped onion
8 tablespoons butter
1½ pounds bulk sausage
4 cups crumbled cornbread
5 cups crumbled bread (white or wheat)
1 cup chopped parsley
2 teaspoons thyme
2 teaspoons sage
1 cup pecans, chopped coarsely
Salt and pepper

1. Rinse and pick over berries. Drain.
2. Sauté onion in butter over low heat for 10-15 minutes, until golden. Transfer to large bowl.
3. Brown sausage in skillet, crumbling finely with fork as it cooks. Transfer to bowl along with hot fat.
4. Add remaining ingredients to bowl and mix. Salt and pepper to taste. Add cranberries. Cool thoroughly before stuffing bird or refrigerate until ready to use. Do not stuff bird until ready to roast.

Fills 18- to 20-pound turkey

CRANBERRY KETCHUP

Karen Malody, a food and restaurant consultant in Seattle, numbers this recipe among the many inventive ones she has developed for clients. It's as versatile as tomato ketchup. Try it as a ham glaze, as a dipping sauce for smoked meats, as an addition to salad dressings or as a warm sauce for poultry or game.

    1 pound cranberries
    1 medium onion, chopped finely
    ½ cup white distilled vinegar
    1 cup sugar
    ¾ teaspoon ground cloves
    ¾ teaspoon ground ginger
    ¾ teaspoon allspice
    ¾ teaspoon salt
    ¾ teaspoon celery seed
    ½ teaspoon pepper

1. Rinse berries under running water. Combine them with onion and ½ cup water in large, noncorrosive pan. Bring to boil, reduce heat to low, cover and simmer 10-12 minutes, or until berries can be mashed against side of pan with spoon.
2. Puree berry mixture, with cooking liquid, through fine blade of food mill or through fine sieve. Discard skins.
3. Return puree to pan and stir in vinegar, sugar, cloves, ginger, allspice, salt, celery seed and pepper. Bring to boil and cook, uncovered, 15 minutes, or until most of the liquid has evaporated and ketchup is thick enough to hold its shape almost solidly in spoon. Stir occasionally to prevent sticking. Skim and discard any foam that appears. Taste and correct seasoning. Cool and refrigerate for early use, or can according to your normal canning procedure.

Makes about 2 cups

STEAMED CRANBERRY PUDDING

Easy, but not quick, this steamed dessert pudding should be served warm. Try it with the simple sauce below.

    2 cups chopped cranberries
    ½ cup molasses
    2 teaspoons baking soda
    ½ cup boiling water
    1½ cups flour

1. Combine cranberries, molasses, soda and boiling water. Stir in flour until mixture is blended.
2. Turn batter into 1-quart buttered pudding mold. Secure lid (or cover with foil secured by string). Place in deep pan. Pour boiling water into pan until it reaches two-thirds up sides of mold. Cover pan and steam pudding over medium-low heat 2½ hours. Remove mold from pan and let stand 15-20 minutes before unmolding pudding by inverting onto plate. Serve pudding warm with vanilla sauce.

Vanilla Sauce

    ½ cup butter
    1 cup sugar
    ½ cup half-and-half
    ¼ teaspoon vanilla

Melt butter in pan, add remaining ingredients and cook, stirring, until hot, but do not boil. Serve warm.
Serves 6-8

CRANBERRY-BREAD PUDDING

This dish is slightly sweet, which makes it a good accompaniment for poultry, ham or pork. It's quick and easy, too.

> 8 ounces tomato sauce
> ¼ cup beef stock
> ¼ cup port
> ¾ cup brown sugar
> 2 tablespoons lemon juice
> 1 tablespoon balsamic vinegar
>   Salt to taste
> 2 cups large bread cubes
> 8 tablespoons butter, melted
> 1 cup cranberries, chopped coarsely

1. Combine all ingredients except bread cubes, melted butter and cranberries. Bring to boil, reduce heat and simmer 5 minutes.
2. Butter a pie dish or shallow casserole. Scatter bread cubes in dish and pour on melted butter. Combine cranberries with sauce. Pour into dish.
3. Bake at 375°F, covered, for 15 minutes. Remove cover and bake 15 minutes more. Serve warm.

Serves 4-6

BLACKBERRY SORBET

Serve this immediately or pour into a mold and freeze for at least 2 hours.

> ⅓ cup crème de cassis
> 1½ tablespoons lemon juice
> ¼ cup sugar
> 1 pound frozen blackberries

Combine crème de cassis, lemon juice and sugar in processor or blender. Add half the berries and process. With machine running, add remaining berries one at a time. Spoon a little additional crème de cassis over each serving.
Serves 4

BLACKBERRY SAUCE FOR STEAMED CAULIFLOWER

This odd combination draws raves at the Mountain Song Restaurant in Marble-mount, at the western end of the North Cascades Highway. One of the restaurant's cooks, Carmen Buchanan, developed it and says the secret to the dish is that the blackberry sauce is unsweetened.

> 1 large cauliflower
> 1 cup blackberries
> ⅓ cup water
> 1 tablespoon cornstarch
> 2 tablespoons water
>   Salt

1. Trim cauliflower and steam it in a covered pot, until barely tender.
2. Meanwhile, prepare sauce by bringing blackberries and ⅓ cup water to boil, reducing heat and simmering 5 minutes. Strain out seeds and return juice to pan. Bring back to boil. Mix cornstarch and 2 tablespoons water, then add mixture to blackberry juice. Stirring, boil 1 minute. Salt to taste.
3. Keep sauce warm until cauliflower is done. Place cauliflower on serving platter and pour on hot sauce.

Serves 4

Note: *For a richer sauce, omit cornstarch and, off heat, swirl 2 tablespoons butter bit by bit into hot sauce.*

BLACKBERRY FLAN

This is a simple dessert most often associated with the cherry season in the French province of Limousin, where it is known as clafouti. It's nothing more than a fruit-filled pancake. This version, with the addition of beaten egg whites, makes a lighter dish. Fresh blueberries or raspberries may be substituted for blackberries. And, of course, fresh sweet cherries may be substituted, also. In the case of cherries, cut back the flour to ²/₃ cup.

> ⅓ cup sugar
> 3 eggs
> 1¼ cups milk
> 1 cup all-purpose flour, sifted
> 1 teaspoon vanilla
> Pinch salt
> 2 egg whites
> 2 cups blackberries
> ⅓ cup sugar
> Powdered sugar

1. Blend, process or beat thoroughly ⅓ cup sugar, eggs, milk, flour, vanilla and salt.
2. Beat egg whites to soft peak and fold into batter.
3. Butter 9-inch, shallow baking dish or pie plate and pour in batter to ¼-inch depth. Place on medium-hot burner for about 90 seconds until batter sets. Remove from heat.
4. Spread berries over batter and sprinkle with the other ⅓ cup sugar. Cover berries with remaining batter and smooth surface.
5. Bake at 350°F for about 1 hour, until flan has browned and knife inserted in center comes out clean.
6. Sprinkle with powdered sugar and serve hot or warm.

Serves 6-8

Note: Unsweetened, frozen berries may be substituted with moderate success. Use about 10 ounces of frozen berries, well drained.

BLACK CURRANT SAUCE

Black currants are strongly flavored. Here's a method of extracting most of the flavor from a supply of the berries, freezing the extract for use in parfaits, mousses, ice creams and so on and still producing an excellent sauce for goose, duck or game.

> 1½ pounds black currants
> Juice of 1 orange
> 2 cups chicken stock
> 1 cup red wine
> Salt and pepper
> 4 tablespoons butter

1. Combine currants with 1 cup water, bring to boil in pan, cover, reduce heat to low and simmer 20-30 minutes, until berries are quite soft.
2. Strain mixture through sieve, but do not press on berries to extract juice. Reserve sludge for sauce. Strain liquid through double thickness of cheesecloth. Cool and freeze the juice for other uses.
3. Return sludge to pan, cover with water, bring to boil, reduce heat and simmer 20-30 minutes. Puree mixture in a processor or blender. Then strain it through sieve, pressing solids with a spoon.
4. Return liquid to pan and boil to reduce to 2 cups.
5. Add orange juice, chicken stock and red wine. Boil to reduce by two-thirds. Salt and pepper to taste. Off heat, whisk in butter bit by bit. Serve warm.

Makes 2¼ cups

RED CURRANT SAUCE

This is one of the sauces Bruce Naftaly serves at his Le Gourmand restaurant in Seattle. Depending, as it does, on a demi-glaze, this is a professional sauce, easy enough for a chef with several helpers, a self-heating stockpot and countless hours available to prepare. Still, a dedicated amateur cook who cares enough to go to the time and expense of preparing this will be rewarded with a rich, glossy sauce of deep color and unsurpassed flavor. Try it with any cut of game or lamb—chops, for instance, that have been sautéed in butter flavored by garlic.

> 3 cups demi-glaze (see below)
> 1½ pounds red currants or ¾ cup red
> currant juice
> ¼ cup crème de cassis or currant eau
> de vie
> Salt and pepper
> 1 tablespoon unsalted butter

1. Simmer demi-glaze with currants or currant juice uncovered for 3 hours or until reduced by two-thirds. Skim carefully. Strain through fine sieve and return to heat.
2. Add cassis. Salt and pepper to taste. Cook for 20 minutes. Just before serving, whisk in the butter.

Demi-Glaze

This is Naftaly's version of the French classic, without the flour thickening. After 24 hours, it will yield about 3 cups of syrupy demi-glaze, enough to be used for the red currant sauce.

> Vegetable oil
> 2 pounds veal, lamb or game bones, cut
> into small pieces
> 2 carrots, chunked
> 1 medium onion, chunked
> ½ stalk celery, chunked
> 1 cup red wine
> 1 cup white wine
> ½ cup Madeira
> 2 bay leaves
> Sprig of thyme (or pinch of dried)
> Sprig of rosemary (or pinch of dried)
> Sprig of marjoram (or pinch of dried)
> Few parsley stems

Note: *To complete, recipe will require three times amounts listed above.*

1. Brown bones over medium-high heat in enough vegetable oil to cover bottom of heavy skillet or large casserole. Scrape pan frequently. Add carrots, onion and celery, and brown.
2. Deglaze pan with wines, scraping bottom and stirring until it is reduced by two-thirds.
3. Reduce heat to low, add herbs and enough cold water to cover ingredients. Simmer slowly, skimming occasionally, with pan half-covered for about 8 hours. Keep replenishing with water as needed to cover ingredients.
4. Strain well, squeezing all the juices out of vegetables.
5. Repeat above procedure, using same amount of ingredients. But this time substitute the first batch of stock for the cold water.
6. Repeat procedure again, using same amount of ingredients. But this time use the stock from the first two batches for the cold water.
7. Reduce stock from all three batches by one-half over medium heat.

Note: *The demi-glaze will keep indefinitely in the refrigerator provided you bring it to a boil once a week; or it will keep indefinitely frozen.*

GOOSEBERRY SAUCE
(For fish)

Bruce Naftaly, of Le Gourmand restaurant in Seattle, is one of Washington's most innovative chefs and a dedicated user of fresh local ingredients. This is his adaptation of a classic British dish that combines the tartness of gooseberries with the oiliness of mackerel. Naftaly, true to his convictions, uses a local fish, lingcod, which he suggests be poached.

4 tablespoons unsalted butter
½ pound gooseberries
2 tablespoons reduced fish stock
¼ cup heavy cream
   Salt and white pepper

1. Melt butter in heavy saucepan, add gooseberries and cook on medium-low heat for 10-15 minutes, until berries can be stirred into a puree.
2. Force berries through a fine sieve. Reduce heat to low and add reduced fish stock and cream. Salt and pepper to taste and heat sauce without boiling. Serve hot over fish.

Poached Lingcod

4 lingcod fillets, about 1½ inches thick
1 leek, chopped coarsely
½ medium onion, chopped coarsely
1 cup white wine

Surround cod with leek and onion in fish poacher. Add wine and water to just cover fish. Bring to bare simmer and cook 15-20 minutes. Fish is done when it feels about half as firm as it was uncooked.

GOOSEBERRY-ORANGE PIE

Most gooseberry fanciers like their pies tart, as this is. You might want to increase the amount of sugar.

4 cups gooseberries
1 cup sugar
3 tablespoons cornstarch
1 tablespoon orange zest
1 tablespoon butter
   Pastry for 2-crust, 9-inch pie
   Cream

1. Rinse, top and tail berries. Mix sugar and cornstarch and pour over berries. Sprinkle mixture with orange zest, then turn into pie shell. Dot berries with butter. Cover with top crust, pinch together sides. Poke holes in top crust or cut out design. Brush top crust with cream.
2. Bake at 400°F for 10 minutes, then reduce heat to 350°F and bake another 40 minutes, until crust is browned and pie juices are slightly thick. Serve warm or cold.

Serves 6-8

CREAMS FOR BERRIES

Berries and cream have a natural affinity.
Plain cream—or crème fraiche (see Notes
on Ingredients, page xi) — can be ideal.
But there are several alternatives, such as
the following.

Zabaione Cream

>   6 *egg yolks*
>   *⅓ cup sugar*
>   *⅔ cup orange-flavored liqueur*
>   *1 cup cream*
>   *2 tablespoons sugar*
>   *3 tablespoons orange-flavored liqueur*

1. Boil water in the bottom of a double
   boiler, making certain the top part
   does not touch the water.
2. Beat the egg yolks with the ⅓ cup sugar
   in a bowl until the sugar is entirely dissolved (this is important) and the mixture becomes light-colored and fluffy.
   Slowly stir in ⅔ cup liqueur. Transfer
   mixture to top of double boiler.
3. Whisk constantly until the mixture
   thickens to the point that it holds its
   shape in a spoon, about 5 minutes. Do
   not allow mixture to boil. Remove
   from heat and whisk 2-3 minutes to
   cool. Lay round of lightly buttered
   waxed paper on surface and refrigerate
   1 hour to cool completely.
4. Whip cream with 2 tablespoons sugar.
   Stir in remaining liqueur. Combine
   with cooled zabaione. Serve chilled.

Sour Cream with Brown Sugar

>   *1½ cups sour cream*
>   *½ cup light brown sugar*
>   *½ tablespoon orange zest*

Combine all ingredients and
serve chilled.

Sour Cream with Whipped Cream

>   *1 cup sour cream*
>   *1 cup lightly whipped cream*
>   *Sugar*

Combine the two creams and sweeten
to taste. Serve chilled.

Mascarpone Cream

>   *3 ounces mascarpone (or cream cheese,*
>   *softened)*
>   *Sugar*
>   *¼ cup cream*
>   *2 tablespoons orange-flavored liqueur*

Beat cheese until creamy. Beat in
sugar to taste. Slowly beat in cream. (Add
more cream if thinner consistency is desired.) Stir in liqueur. Serve chilled.

BIVALVES

No statue rises, no plaque gleams, but somewhere there ought to be a commemorative to the unknown oyster eater, that proverbial fellow of unsurpassed courage who first dared swallow one of the cold, slippery little animals.

Washington would be as good a place as any to note that milestone in culinary history. Washed by cold Pacific waters, blessed by Puget Sound's placid bays and inlets, Washington provides a perfect habitat for oysters—and for many other bivalves, including this planet's most spectacular clam, the giant geoduck.

Bivalves are easily distinguished from other shellfish. They are those marine animals with two shells, two "valves." From a gustatory standpoint, three of Washington's stand out: oysters, mussels and clams. All three are also important economically, especially oysters and mussels, of which Washington ranks as the Pacific Coast's leading producer.

Oysters played a significant role in Washington's early history, helping to spread the Puget Sound region's reputation as a horn of plenty. Great oyster beds greeted the first settlers. These were the West Coast's only native oysters, the so-called "western" oysters or, as they became known, Olympias. Tiny, flavored by the essence of the sea, Olympia oysters gained great favor in the mid-19th-century saloons and the plush dining rooms of gold-fevered San Francisco, though it's doubtful they arrived there in prime condition. Unfortunately, Olympias were so easily harvested that they soon became scarce. Later, pollution from lumber mills nearly finished them off. Today, Olympias are making a comeback, thanks to the determined efforts of a few growers. They are not readily available, however, and those that do reach the market are usually sold to restaurants.

Faced with the dramatic decline of the native oyster, Puget Sound's oystermen turned to Japan at the beginning of this century and imported seed of what is now known as the Pacific oyster. Much larger and less distinctive in taste than the Olympia, the Pacific oyster thrives in Washington's waters and today is nearly the only oyster found here.

Like wine grapes, oysters take on the qualities of their growing conditions. Selecting them, particularly for eating raw, is as tricky and susceptible to individual preference as is choosing a wine. For cooking, the choice of oysters is less important. Make certain they're fresh and buy oysters in the jar only as a last resort.

Raw oysters are not to everyone's taste. Given a supply of fresh oysters in the shell, one easy method of preparing them favored

OYSTER SOUP

The best oyster soup consists of butter, cream and the oysters themselves. This might be second best.

2 cups clam juice
6 cups fish stock
2 dozen small shucked oysters
1 cup white wine
8 tablespoons butter
1 onion, chopped finely
2 leeks (white part only), chopped finely
3 tablespoons flour
2 cloves garlic, chopped
½ pound sorrel, in ½-inch cross-slices
¼ pound spinach, shredded
2 potatoes, in small dice
3 egg yolks
1 cup cream
    Lemon juice
    Salt and pepper

1. Bring clam juice, fish stock, oysters' liquor and wine to boil, reduce heat and simmer 10 minutes.
2. Melt 6 tablespoons of the butter in soup pot. Sauté onion and leeks over low heat 10-12 minutes, until limp but not brown. Sprinkle vegetables with flour and cook, stirring, about 3 minutes, until flour disappears. Off heat, add fish liquids. Bring to boil, reduce heat and simmer, partly covered, 10 minutes.
3. Meanwhile, sauté garlic in remaining butter until light gold. Add sorrel and spinach and sauté until limp. Add to soup, along with potatoes. Simmer until potatoes are tender.
4. Beat egg yolks with cream. Mix ¼ cup of hot soup into the cream mixture and then pour all into soup, stirring until it thickens.
5. Add oysters and lemon juice to taste. Salt and pepper to taste. Simmer just long enough to heat oysters through. Serve immediately.

Serves 6

OYSTER LOAF

Here's an excellent method of converting ordinary or jarred oysters into a tasty dish for lunch or a picnic.

1 large oblong loaf of Italian or
    French bread
1 sweet red pepper, diced finely
2 tomatoes, diced finely and drained
6 anchovy fillets, minced
½ cup oil-cured olives, pitted and chopped
½ cup black olives, pitted and chopped
½ medium onion, diced finely
4 cloves garlic, minced
2 tablespoons capers, rinsed and drained
2 tablespoons chopped fresh basil
2 tablespoons chopped fresh parsley
1 tablespoon lemon juice
1 tablespoon red wine vinegar
2 tablespoons olive oil
2 cups shucked oysters
½ cup grated Parmesan
    Salt and pepper

1. Slice bread in half lengthwise and scoop out insides. Process or chop scooped-out bread into crumbs.
2. Combine all ingredients except oysters and Parmesan.
3. Poach oysters in 2 cups simmering fish stock or 1½ cups water and ½ cup dry vermouth 3-4 minutes. Drain, cool and chop coarsely. Combine with bread crumb mixture. Mix in Parmesan. Salt and pepper to taste.
4. Brush insides of hollowed-out bread loaf halves lightly with olive oil. Fill halves with oyster mixture, packing firmly. Re-form loaf by joining halves, wrap tightly with foil and refrigerate at least overnight. Slice to serve.

Serves 6-8

Steve Jones gathering mussels on Puget Sound.

by people who don't like raw oysters or who shun shucking is to place them on a grill over the embers of a wood fire or under a broiler and simply wait for them to open up. Napped with melted butter or a squeeze of lemon juice, broiled oysters are a tasty alternative to raw.

Incidentally, it isn't true that eating oysters harvested in months without an *r* will make you sick. But it is true that oysters are nowhere near their peak during those summer months because warm water triggers their spawning cycle; they become soft, milky and thin. Two University of

Washington graduate students, however, have developed a method of sexually confusing oysters so they remain plump and crisp during what would be their spawning time. As commercial oystermen adopt the practice, summer oysters will become as delectable as winter oysters.

Unlike oysters, mussels are pretty much a recent addition to Washington's dining tables. Though wild mussels were found throughout Washington's waters when settlers arrived, they were largely ignored. It wasn't until the first cultivated mussels appeared in the mid-1970s that

FRIED OYSTERS WITH REMOULADE SAUCE

Hank Odland, of Hank's by the Lake in Seattle, fries oysters as well as anyone. Here's his secret, and a recipe for a gussied-up tartar sauce with a French name.

1 cup flour
1 tablespoon dried dill
1 tablespoon dried thyme
Pinch salt
Pinch white pepper
2 dozen small oysters, shucked
Beer
2 cups panko (Japanese rice breading)
Peanut or soybean oil
Remoulade sauce (see below)

1. Mix flour, dill, thyme, salt and white pepper. Dip oysters in mixture and shake off excess.
2. Dip oysters in beer and then in panko, shaking them to thoroughly coat.
3. Heat ¼ inch or so of the oil to 375°F in a skillet. Fry oysters 1-2 minutes to brown, flip and brown other side. Do not overcook or oysters will become tough. Serve hot with remoulade.

Serves 4

Remoulade Sauce

2 cups mayonnaise
4 tablespoons minced dill pickles
4 tablespoons capers, rinsed, drained and chopped
1 teaspoon minced parsley
1 teaspoon minced fresh tarragon
1 teaspoon minced fresh chives
½ teaspoon anchovy paste

Combine all ingredients and chill.

BAKED OYSTERS WITH MUSHROOM BUTTER

Serve these with a good bread and a crisp white wine.

3 dozen oysters, on half-shell
1 pound butter
1 bunch parsley
1 cup mushrooms
6 cloves garlic
4 shallots
½ cup chopped ham
Salt and pepper
Lemon wedges

Topping

1 cup dried bread crumbs
2 tablespoons olive oil
2 tablespoons grated Parmesan

1. Pour liquor off oysters and reserve for another use.
2. Prepare mushroom butter by first combining all remaining ingredients except lemon wedges in processor, then processing until blended.
3. Prepare the topping by moistening bread crumbs with olive oil and mixing with Parmesan.
4. Set oysters on rock salt (to keep them level) in roasting pan. Top each with gob of mushroom butter and sprinkle of topping. Preheat oven to 450°F. Place oysters in oven, turn heat down to 350°F and bake 10 minutes. Finish by browning topping under broiler. Serve immediately with lemon wedges.

Serves 3-6

Washington cooks began to appreciate them. Today, mussels are readily available year-round in many fish markets and on restaurant menus.

Washington mussels and those from the East Coast are the same species, the blue mussel. They differ in appearance and taste, however, because of water and harvesting conditions. East Coast mussels are dredged from the sea bottom; they tend to be older, larger and more salmon-colored. Washington mussels that reach the market are all cultivated—grown clinging to ropes suspended beneath log rafts. Consequently, they're younger than their East Coast cousins. They also are creamier-colored, plumper and milder in flavor. The center of mussel production on the entire West Coast is the long bay called Penn Cove on Whidbey Island. Penn Cove mussels are so superior to East Coast mussels that the continued presence of the imported mussels in Washington can only be attributed to old-fashioned snobbery.

Among the many clams found in Washington, the gastronomic favorite clearly is the razor clam, which thrives most abundantly in the sandy beaches of southwestern Washington. Commercial harvesting of razor clams is severely restricted because they draw such heavy attention from sport clammers.

Clams most widely available to both commercial and sport clammers are the so-called steamer clams, of which three, the native littleneck, the butter and the Manila, are the most important. Manila clams, which are not native but came to Washington accidentally along with shipments of Japanese oyster seed, account for over half the commercial haul and are the most common clams found in markets.

As with all the bivalves, clams whose shells are open or broken should not be cooked and eaten. One test is to try to slide a clam's shell apart between your fingers. A clam opening in this manner should be discarded. Bivalves that fail to open during cooking should also be discarded.

Finally, there is the glorious geoduck, the largest clam in the world, which is found from Alaska to California. However, it grows in great numbers only in Puget Sound and certain inland waters of British Columbia. Geoducks sold in markets average about two to three pounds, but this giant has been known to reach an incredible 13 pounds, bigger than most newborn babies.

A geoduck's size alone marks it as special. But Washingtonians also delight in its name, "gooey-duck," which is thought to be of Indian origin. (Spellings vary—*geoduck, goiduck, gweduck*—but geoduck has become standard.) Though geoducks are imposing, their meat actually is quite delicately flavored, and most of the commercially taken geoducks end up in canned clam chowder.

Cleaning a geoduck is easier than it sounds. Drop it in boiling water for about 10 seconds. Using a small knife, remove the clam from the shell and pare the viscera away from the breast (mantle) and the neck (siphon). Peel the skin off the neck and breast; it should slip away easily. Wash the meat, then slit the neck lengthwise and wash away any grit.

Both neck and breast meat may be chopped for chowder. They also may be sliced into steaks and eaten raw, as in sashimi or sushi. The Japanese are great fanciers of geoduck and prefer neck steaks because that meat is crisper. The Chinese prefer tender breast steaks for sautéing. Neck steaks are equally as good for sautéing, but they should be pounded gently to tenderize them.

OYSTER, BEEF AND BOURBON STEW

Diamond Jim Brady would have loved this robust dish.

    1 pound slab bacon in ½-inch dice
    4 pounds trimmed stewing beef chunks
        Salt and pepper
    ½ cup bourbon
    1 carrot, in 1-inch pieces
    1 onion, chopped
    2 stalks celery in 1 inch pieces
    1 potato, peeled and chunked
    3 tablespoons tomato sauce
    1 bay leaf
    3 cloves garlic, peeled
    ¼ teaspoon thyme
    6 cups beef stock
    2-3 dozen shucked oysters
        Steak sauce
        Tabasco

1. Brown bacon dice in large skillet over low heat. Remove bacon and reserve.
2. Pat beef chunks dry, lightly salt and pepper and brown in bacon fat. Pour bourbon over beef and flame. Remove beef and reserve. Pour fat from skillet.
3. Return bacon and beef to skillet. Add all other ingredients except oysters and sauces. Bring to boil, cover and simmer until beef is tender, 2-3 hours, adding boiling water if necessary.
4. Remove bacon and beef from skillet. Discard bay leaf. Puree vegetables with liquid in blender or processor. Return to skillet with bacon and beef. Add steak sauce and Tabasco to taste.
5. Just before serving, reheat stew to simmer, add oysters along with their liquor and heat until oysters' edges curl. Serve immediately.

Serves 4-8

MARINATED OYSTERS

Of the hundreds of oyster recipes developed over the years at The Oyster Bar on Chuckanut Drive south of Bellingham, this one draws as many raves as any. The amount given here is ample to serve eight as a first course, but the leftovers may be kept in the refrigerator for several days.

    1 quart extra-small oysters
    1½ cups white wine
    ⅓ cup red wine vinegar
    ½ cup olive oil
    ⅔ cup lemon juice
    ½ teaspoon salt
    ½ teaspoon pepper
    ½ teaspoon thyme
    ½ teaspoon chervil
    2 tablespoons minced parsley
    1 tablespoon minced garlic
    ½ cup diced red onions
    2 teaspoons minced fresh chives

1. In a noncorrosive pan, combine all ingredients, including oysters, and let stand 15-20 minutes.
2. Over low heat, bring marinade with oysters in it to bare simmer, just to poach oysters lightly. Remove from heat and immediately transfer oysters and marinade to cold bowl. Chill in refrigerator for at least several hours.
3. Serve oysters on lettuce with some of the onions and a bit of marinade.

Serves 8

Oysters,
Beef and
Bourbon
Stew

Marinated
Oysters

CLAM SOUP

Here's an alternative to clam chowder.

   3 dozen clams, scrubbed
 ½ cup white wine
   6 tablespoons butter
 ¼ cup minced onion
 ½ pound mushrooms, sliced thinly
   3 tablespoons flour
   4 cups chicken stock
   1 cup tiny peas
 ½ cup cream

1. Steam clams with wine and 3 tablespoons of the butter until they open. (Discard clams that don't open.) Remove clams from shells. Strain clam broth through cheesecloth. Reserve.
2. Saute onions in remaining butter over low heat 6-7 minutes. Add mushrooms, increase heat to medium-high and cook until their liquid has evaporated. Sprinkle with flour and cook, stirring, until flour has disappeared. Transfer to soup pot.
3. Add hot chicken stock and clam broth. Bring to boil, stirring, and simmer 10 minutes.
4. Meanwhile, simmer peas separately until tender. Add peas, cream and clams to soup and heat through. Serve immediately.

Serves 4-6

CLAMS IN BLACK BEAN SAUCE

As Chinese as it sounds, this dish is aromatic and strongly flavored. Serve as a main course with steamed rice.

   3 dozen clams, scrubbed
   3 tablespoons vegetable oil
   1 tablespoon Chinese fermented black
      beans
   2 cloves garlic, sliced
   2 teaspoons minced fresh ginger
 ½ teaspoon Chinese chili paste (optional)
   1 tablespoon sherry
   1 tablespoon soy sauce
   1 tablespoon Chinese oyster sauce
 ½ cup chicken stock
   2 teaspoons sugar
    Pinch pepper
   1 scallion, chopped finely
   1 tablespoon cornstarch
   1 tablespoon water
   1 teaspoon sesame oil

1. Steam clams, covered, in small amount of water until they open. (Discard clams that don't open.) Drain clams. Reserve in shells.
2. In wok, or large skillet, heat oil and swirl to coat sides. Add black beans, garlic, ginger and chili paste. Stir-fry 30 seconds. Add clams, sherry, soy sauce, oyster sauce, chicken stock, sugar and pepper. Stir gently, then cover and steam 1 minute. Uncover and stir in scallion, cooking 1 minute more. Mix cornstarch and water to make paste. Stir in, a little at a time, until sauce thickens. Sprinkle with sesame oil and serve immediately.

Serves 4-6

CLAM SAUCE FOR PASTA

Is there a more popular pasta sauce? This one is simple, as a clam sauce should be.

 ¼ cup minced onion
 ½ cup olive oil
 1 teaspoon finely chopped garlic
 3 dozen clams, scrubbed
 ½ cup white wine
 3 tablespoons butter, at room
 temperature
 Clam juice
 1 pound spaghettini or linguine
 2 tablespoons chopped parsley

1. Bring large pot of salted water to boil for pasta.
2. Meanwhile, in skillet with tight-fitting lid, sauté onion in olive oil over medium-low heat 5 minutes, until limp but not brown. Increase heat slightly and add garlic, cooking until it begins to color. Add clams and wine. Add 1 tablespoon of the butter, cover and steam until clams just open. Remove from heat immediately. (Discard clams that don't open.) When clams are cool enough to handle, remove 2 dozen from their shells, reserving the other dozen, covered and warm, as a garnish.
3. Strain clam broth from skillet through layers of cheesecloth. Add clam juice to broth to make 1¼ cups. Boil to reduce to ¾ cup. Keep hot.
4. Cook pasta according to package directions. Drain and transfer to a warm bowl.
5. Toss pasta with remaining butter. Add hot clam broth and clams. Sprinkle with parsley and toss. Serve pasta immediately with clams in their shells as garnish.
Serves 4

CLAM HASH

Though it's been said of Emmett Watson, the eminent Seattle newspaper columnist and stalwart friend of the authors, that he never met a meal he didn't like, he does have certain preferences. Among them are clams and potatoes, which he combines in this dish.

 6 slices bacon
 4 tablespoons butter
 2 shallots, chopped finely
 ½ small onion, chopped finely
 2½ cups diced boiled potatoes
 2½ cups minced clams
 Salt and pepper
 4 egg yolks
 ¾ cup cream
 2 tablespoons softened butter

1. Sauté bacon in heavy skillet over low heat until crisp. Drain and crumble. Pour off bacon fat and melt butter in skillet. Sauté shallots and onion 7-8 minutes, until soft.
2. Add potatoes, increase heat to medium and cook until underside is browned. Mix in clams and bacon. Salt and pepper to taste.
3. Cook mixture 2-3 minutes. Press flat with spatula.
4. Beat egg yolks with cream. Pour mixture over clam-potato mixture. Cover skillet and cook about 3 minutes, until eggs are just set.
5. Dot hash with softened butter. Brown under broiler. Serve immediately.
Serves 4-6

CLAMS TRIESTE

Eaten with lots of crusty bread and a crisp white wine or full-flavored beer, this dish becomes either a light meal or a memorable first course.

6 dozen medium steamer clams, scrubbed
1 cup dry vermouth
2 teaspoons lemon pepper

Sauce

½ cup coarsely chopped onions
6 cloves garlic, minced
  Olive oil
1 cup parsley
1 scallion
  Pinch rosemary
  Pinch tarragon
  Pinch marjoram
1 teaspoon Worcestershire sauce
1 teaspoon English mustard
1 teaspoon brandy
1 tablespoon Madeira
2 teaspoons lemon juice
½ pound unsalted butter, softened
3 anchovy fillets, chopped
½ teaspoon salt
  Pepper
1 egg

1. Prepare sauce first. Sauté onion and garlic quickly in a little olive oil without letting them color. Place in bowl of food processor along with parsley, scallion, rosemary, tarragon and marjoram. Process thoroughly.
2. Add Worcestershire sauce, mustard, brandy, Madeira and lemon juice. Process until well blended. Remove to bowl and clean processor bowl.
3. Process butter for 2 minutes. Add anchovies and process until well blended. Add other mixture and process 10 seconds. Add salt, pepper and egg. Process another 10 seconds.
4. To prepare clams, place them in heavy pot with vermouth and lemon pepper. Cover tightly and cook over medium heat until clams open, 4 to 6 minutes. (Discard clams that don't open.)
5. To assemble, remove top shells of clams. Place clams in oven-proof dishes or in large pan. Top with generous dabs of sauce. Place on top shelf of 500°F oven and bake until bubbly, 6-7 minutes. Serve immediately.

Serves 6-12

MUSSEL SALAD

For mussel fanciers, here's a contemporary method of serving the plump bivalves.

3 dozen mussels, scrubbed and debearded
½ cup white wine
1 tablespoon butter
2 sprigs parsley, minced
2 cups peeled, seeded and diced
  cucumber

Sauce

6 tablespoons spicy brown mustard
2 teaspoons Dijon-style mustard
3 tablespoons white wine vinegar
3 tablespoons sugar
  Salt and pepper
½ cup vegetable oil
½ cup minced fresh dill

1. Steam mussels, covered, with wine, butter and parsley 3-5 minutes, until they open. (Discard mussels that don't open.) Drain and remove from shells.
2. Prepare sauce by mixing mustards with vinegar, sugar and salt and pepper. Gradually whisk in the oil and dill.
3. Combine mussels, cucumber dice and sauce and toss. Serve on a bed of shredded salad greens.

Serves 4-6

MUSSELS WITH ORANGE MAYONNAISE

Luciano Bardinelli, the owner and some-time chef of the trailblazing Northern Italian restaurant in Seattle called Settebello, often favors his guests in warm weather with this appetizer.

> 2 dozen large mussels, scrubbed and debearded
> 1 orange
> 3 tablespoons mayonnaise

1. Place mussels in heavy pot, cover tightly and cook over medium heat 5-6 minutes, until mussels open. (Discard mussels that don't open.) Drain mussels, detach from shells, then replace in shells and chill briefly.
2. Peel orange without cutting into the white pith underneath. Slice peel into thin strips. Drop strips into boiling water for 2 minutes. Drain and cool.
3. Combine mayonnaise and juice of orange. Dab sauce on mussels in their shells, garnish with orange peel and serve cold.

Serves 4-6

CREAM OF MUSSEL SOUP

This is a delicious variation on a classic French soup.

> 2 pounds mussels, scrubbed and debearded
> 2 shallots, chopped
> 2 small onions, chopped
> Several sprigs parsley
> 1 cup dry white wine
> 2 tablespoons butter
> 1 bay leaf
> Salt and pepper
> 2 cups cream
> ½ teaspoon stem saffron
> 1 egg yolk, beaten

1. Place mussels in heavy pot along with shallots, onions, parsley, wine, butter, bay leaf and salt and pepper. Bring to boil and simmer until mussels open, about 6 minutes.
2. Strain contents of pot through cheesecloth or fine sieve. Discard mussels.
3. Bring strained liquid to boil. Add cream and saffron. Bring to boil again. Remove pot from heat and stir in egg. Return to heat and stir as soup thickens slightly. Do not boil. Serve hot or cold.

Serves 4-6

STEAMED MUSSELS

A simple potion, but powerfully good with crusty bread to sop up the liquid.

> 1 medium onion, chopped
> 4 cloves garlic, minced
> ½ cup olive oil
> 1 cup white wine
> Pepper
> 2 pounds fresh tomatoes, peeled and chopped (or 2 cups canned)
> 2 tablespoons finely chopped basil (or 1 tablespoon dried)
> 4 pounds mussels, scrubbed and debearded
> 2 teaspoons minced lemon zest
> 2 tablespoons chopped parsley

1. Sauté onion and garlic in olive oil 10 minutes, in large casserole or pan with tight-fitting lid.
2. Add wine and boil 3 minutes, until liquid is reduced by half. Pepper to taste. Add tomatoes and their liquid and basil. Simmer 20 minutes while stirring occasionally.
3. Add mussels, cover and steam over high heat to open, about 10 minutes, shaking pan occasionally. (Discard mussels that don't open.)
4. Ladle into soup plates and sprinkle with lemon zest and parsley. Serve immediately.

Serves 6

SAUTÉED GEODUCK

Francois Kissel, the eminent chef and owner of Seattle's Brasserie Pavillon and Maximilien-in-the-Market, developed this incomparable recipe for sautéing geoduck steaks. It is also a delicious way to prepare razor clams.

> 2 geoducks, about 2 pounds each
> 3 eggs
> Vegetable oil, preferably peanut
> 4 tablespoons unsalted butter, clarified
> Salt and pepper
> Flour.
> Garlic butter (see below)
> White wine
> Lemon

1. Clean geoducks, slice steaks from neck and breast. Pound steaks to tenderize.
2. Whip eggs with 3 tablespoons vegetable oil to make batter. Salt and pepper batter to taste.
3. In heavy skillet, heat equal amounts clarified butter and vegetable oil until quite hot but not smoking.
4. Salt and pepper geoduck steaks to taste. Dredge in flour on both sides. Shake off excess flour, then dip steaks in batter and sauté briefly on both sides until brown. Set steaks aside on hot platter.
5. Clean skillet and return to heat. Add 4-5 tablespoons garlic butter and heat until foaming. Remove from heat and stir in 4-5 teaspoons white wine and a couple of squeezes of lemon juice. Pour sauce over geoduck steaks and serve immediately.

Serves 4-6

Note: Garlic butter can be prepared in advance in any amount, wrapped tightly in foil, frozen and used as needed. Figure about 1 clove garlic and several sprigs of parsley per ¼ pound of unsalted butter, depending on taste. Mince the garlic and parsley. Soften the butter to room temperature and beat ingredients together.

CURRIED SEAFOOD SALAD

The dressing is the key to this salad. What it covers is up to you—and the season. A mixture of clams, mussels, bay scallops and shrimp is ideal. Steam the clams and mussels open in a covered pan with a little water, discarding those that don't open. Boil the shrimp and scallops until they are barely done, peeling the shrimp. Chopped vegetables may be added, as well—bulb fennel and cucumbers, for instance, and tomatoes and scallions.

Dressing

> 1 small onion, minced
> 2 cloves garlic, minced
> 2 tablespoons olive oil
> 1½ tablespoons curry powder
> 6 ounces tomato juice
> Salt and pepper
> 3 slices lemon
> 1 cup mayonnaise
> 1 tablespoon apricot jam

1. Sauté onion and garlic in olive oil over low heat until limp, 10-12 minutes. Add curry powder and cook, stirring, 3 minutes. Add tomato juice. Simmer 10 minutes. Salt and pepper to taste and add lemon slices. Simmer 2 minutes. Strain liquid through layers of cheesecloth. Cool and mix in mayonnaise and apricot jam.
2. Toss with seafood and vegetables, if desired, and chill before serving.

Makes 1¾ cups

CHICKEN

CHICKEN

Compared to Southern states and California, Washington does not grow an especially large number of chickens. Commercial chicken growers here, in fact, produce enough to satisfy only about 45 percent of the state's demand. So what's this chapter doing in a book about foods that flourish in Washington?

Well, when it comes to chickens, freshness is of paramount importance. And the only way a Washington consumer is going to get a fresh chicken is to buy a home-grown one. That fact alone merits the inclusion of chickens in this book, but there's more. Washington chickens are of excellent quality, superior in many ways to chickens shipped in from other states. Small as it is compared to that in some other states, Washington's chicken industry still grows about 22 million birds annually. So a few words about Washington chickens are well in order.

Early in this century, pork consumption far outstripped beef consumption in America. But beef became Americans' first choice in meats as people grew wealthier, beef was more readily available, and certain social changes took place. Today, the trend is toward chicken, and some forecasters are saying that chicken consumption will exceed that of beef by the end of the century. Health concerns explain part of this. Cost concerns explain part, too, for the price of chickens, holding steady as most other prices rise, makes the world's most common fowl the best bargain in the meat case.

Consumer preference in chickens varies around the country, perhaps having more to do with advertising than taste. In Washington, most consumers seem to prefer "white" chickens as opposed to "yellow." So the three big chicken processors in the state send white chickens to market. Whether white chickens taste better than yellow, or even taste different, is arguable. A white chicken has been fed a more varied grain diet than corn-fed yellow birds and has been scalded at a hotter temperature during processing, resulting in the removal of the thin yellow film under the feathers that all chickens have. Aside from color, the film has another important effect. It retains water, which is why many processors in other states don't want to lose it. More moisture means more money for less chicken.

Washington processors can't compete with Southern processors on the basis of price. Everything, from chicken houses to labor to feed, costs less in the South. So they compete on the basis of quality and fair value. They and their contract growers feed, care for and handle their chickens better than most Southern processors do.

POLLO TONNATO

Here's a poultry version of Italy's famous *vitello tonnato*, or cold veal in tuna sauce. It's ideal in the summer.

4 whole chicken breasts (8 halves)
4 quarts chicken stock
3-ounce can Italian tuna in olive oil
¾ cup olive oil
2 egg yolks
4 anchovy fillets, drained and chopped
2 tablespoons lemon juice
    Dash Tabasco
    Salt and pepper
¼ cup cream
3 tablespoons capers, rinsed and drained

Garnishes

Chopped parsley
Italian-style black olives
Thin lemon slices

1. Halve the chicken breasts. Bring chicken stock to boil, add breasts and simmer, partially covered, 15 minutes. Remove from heat and let breasts cool in stock.
2. Drain tuna and add its oil to the olive oil to make 1 cup. Process or blend egg yolks, anchovies, lemon juice and Tabasco 15 seconds. With machine still running, pour in oils in thin, steady stream. Flake tuna and add to sauce. Salt and pepper to taste. Process until well blended. Remove to bowl and stir in cream. (Add poaching liquid as needed to thin sauce to the consistency of heavy cream.) Stir in the capers.
3. Remove breasts from cold stock. (Reserve stock for another use.) Skin and bone breasts. Slice breasts in half horizontally. Spread bottom of serving dish with thin layer of sauce. Lay chicken on top. Pour remainder of sauce over, spreading to mask each piece. Cover with plastic wrap and refrigerate overnight.
4. Serve cold with garnishes.

Serves 6-8

CHICKEN GALANTINE

An elegant first course or buffet dish, this galantine goes especially well with mustard sauce (see page 7).

1 whole chicken
½ pound Italian sausage
½ cup minced onion
3 tablespoons butter
1 cup cream
    Salt and pepper
⅓ cup pistachio nuts, shelled
1 tablespoon fresh minced herbs, such as tarragon, oregano and sage
    Vegetable oil
¼ pound mortadella, sliced thinly

1. Remove skin from chicken in one piece, being careful not to tear. Reserve skin.
2. Remove breast, thigh and drumstick meat from chicken and grind in processor or grinder. Remove casing from sausages and mix the meat with the chicken.
3. Sauté onion in butter over low heat 10-12 minutes without browning. Mix with meat. Stir in cream. Salt and pepper to taste. Fold in pistachio nuts and herbs.
4. Brush one side of 20-inch heavy-duty foil strip with vegetable oil. Set aside. Spread out chicken skin. Cover skin with mortadella slices. Mound meat mixture across middle of mortadella in 3-inch-wide strip the length of the longer dimension of skin. Leave 1-inch border of skin at each end. Roll up firmly into shape of sausage. Wrap roll tightly in oiled foil.
5. Place galantine on baking sheet and bake at 375°F for 1 hour, turning once during baking. Let stand 30 minutes before removing foil, slicing and serving. Better yet, refrigerate 2-3 days in foil before serving.

Serves 6-8

Raising chickens on a Palouse farm.

And they remove the yellow film.

Washington's chicken industry sells "fryers" more or less exclusively. ("Broiler" is the term more common in the East.) A fryer is about seven weeks old and weighs about three and one-half pounds dressed.

Lately, some chicken fanciers have taken to "free-range" chickens on the assumption that such chickens are more "natural," less industrial birds of fuller flavor and better texture. Doubtless such chickens exist. But there are no standards for "free-range" chickens, and as often as not they can be tough, dry, stringy and less flavorful than chickens which are raised in large houses with wood shavings on the floor and are fed in a controlled manner.

Consumer preference rules on this question, as it should. Some people prefer "roasters," which are older and larger than fryers. For some uses, such as flavoring soup or stock, tough old stewing chickens from egg-laying flocks are in fact the most desirable.

For freshness, though, Washington chickens are unsurpassed. Washington processors deliver their chickens to market about 14 hours after processing, without freezing them. Out-of-state chickens are "deep-chilled," which is another way of saying lightly frozen.

It's not easy to spot a fresh chicken, particularly when it's packaged. Look for unbruised birds with clear skin and fresh-looking bones where they're exposed. Slick skin and brown bone-ends signify that a chicken's been around for a while. Smelling a chicken, if that's possible, helps, too. A bird too long in the meat case gives off a distinctive aroma of age.

A fresh chicken not only has better flavor, but also will be moister when it's cooked—that is, if it's not overcooked. Pushed by cooking authorities, people seem to be accepting the idea that they shouldn't overcook chickens if they want the best flavor and the most moisture. "Just until the pinkness is gone" is the operative phrase, and some professional cooks argue that a hint of pinkness should actually be retained. Certainly, long cooking isn't necessary to achieve tenderness in young Washington fryers. Slightly undercooking them, in fact, yields a better texture without stringiness.

CHICKEN-PASTA SALAD

Colorful and flavorful, this salad also can be made with poached chicken breasts rather than the whole chicken called for in this recipe.

> 1 whole chicken
> 1 pound pasta, such as seashells or
>   corkscrews
> 2 tablespoons olive oil
> ½ cup chicken stock (from poaching)
> 1 sweet red pepper, chopped coarsely
> 1 bunch scallions, sliced thinly
> ½ cup capers, rinsed and drained
> ½ cup chopped cured black olives
> 1 cup shredded fresh basil (or chopped
>   parsley)
>   Salt and pepper
>   Creamy vinaigrette (see below)

1. Poach room-temperature chicken in enough boiling water to submerge. Boil 30 minutes, turn off heat and let chicken remain in water 20 minutes more. Remove from water and let cool enough to handle. Pull meat from bones and shred into bite-size pieces.
2. Prepare chicken stock by adding chicken bones to poaching liquid, along with 1 chopped onion, 1 chopped carrot, ½ stalk celery, a few sprigs of parsley, ½ teaspoon thyme and a few peppercorns. Salt lightly. Simmer 30-60 minutes. Strain, return to heat and boil to reduce by one-third. Reserve excess stock for another use.
3. Cook pasta in boiling, salted water. Drain and rinse quickly in cold water. Drain again. Toss with olive oil and ½ cup chicken stock. Set aside at room temperature, stirring occasionally, for 20-30 minutes.
4. Mix all other ingredients with pasta. Toss with desired amount of creamy vinaigrette.

Serves 4-6

Creamy Vinaigrette

> 2 egg yolks
> 2 teaspoons Dijon-style mustard
> 1 clove garlic, minced
> ½ teaspoon minced fresh coriander
> ¼ cup red wine vinegar
>   Salt and pepper
> 1 cup olive oil

Whip egg yolks until frothy. Beat in all other ingredients except oil. Whip in oil little by little.

STUFFED CHICKEN BREASTS

This dish goes together easily. It can be served hot as a main course or cold as part of a buffet.

> 2 chicken breasts, left whole
> 8 thin slices prosciutto
> 2 tablespoons pesto (see page 102)
> 2 tablespoons pine nuts
>   Salt and pepper

1. Bone chicken breasts and remove skin and cartilage. Between sheets of waxed paper, gently pound thicker parts of breasts to produce evenly thick fillets. With outer side down, place 4 prosciutto slices on each of the breasts. Spread the prosciutto with pesto and pine nuts. Salt and pepper to taste.
2. Beginning with widest part, roll up each breast into tight cylinder. Place in middle of an oiled square of foil with shiny side up. Tuck one edge of foil tightly under chicken cylinder and then roll up chicken tightly in foil, twisting ends to seal and compact chicken within foil even tighter.
3. Place foil rolls on baking sheet and bake at 400°F for 15 minutes. Remove from oven and let rest 10 minutes. If serving hot, remove foil, slice diagonally and serve immediately. If serving cold, refrigerate in foil.

Serves 4-6

CHICKEN ESCABECHE

This dish can be served for lunch on a warm day or as part of a buffet.

      3 *whole chicken breasts (6 halves)*
        Salt and pepper
        Flour
    ¾ *cup olive oil*
      1 *onion, sliced thinly*
      1 *carrot, sliced thinly*
    ½ *stalk celery, sliced thinly*
      6 *cloves garlic, peeled and sliced*
    ½ *teaspoon thyme*
    10 *whole black peppercorns*
      1 *tablespoon salt*
      1 *sweet red pepper, sliced*
      1 *green pepper, sliced*
      1 *cup chicken stock*
    ½ *cup red wine vinegar*
    ½ *cup white wine*
      2 *bay leaves*

Garnishes

    Chopped parsley
    Cured black olives
    Lemon wedges

1. Bone chicken breasts and remove skin and cartilage. Between sheets of waxed paper, gently pound thicker parts of breasts to produce evenly thick fillets.
2. Salt and pepper breasts lightly, dredge in flour and shake off excess. Sauté in ¼ cup of the olive oil until barely done. (Do not overcook.) Transfer to glass or ceramic dish in one layer.
3. Remove any burnt oil or flour from sauté pan. Add remaining olive oil and over low heat, sauté onion, carrot, celery, garlic, thyme, peppercorns and salt until onions are wilted, 8-10 minutes. (Do not brown.) Add peppers and sauté while stirring 2 minutes more. Add stock, vinegar, wine and bay leaves. Cover and simmer gently 20 minutes.
4. Pour hot marinade over chicken breasts, spreading vegetables evenly. Cool to room temperature and refrigerate at least 24 hours.
5. Serve at room temperature with garnishes.

Serves 4-6

HOT CHICKEN SALAD

This is a Chinese preparation.

      1 *whole chicken*
      1 *small head Romaine lettuce*
        (or watercress)
      4 *tablespoons soy sauce*
      1 *tablespoon vinegar*
      2 *tablespoons corn syrup*
      2 *cloves garlic, minced*
      1 *teaspoon salt*
      3 *tablespoons peanut oil*
      4 *scallions, sliced thinly*
      1 *tablespoon finely chopped fresh ginger*
      1 *teaspoon Sichuan peppercorns, crushed*
    ½ *teaspoon chili oil*
      1 *tablespoon sesame oil*

1. Poach room-temperature chicken in enough boiling water to submerge. Boil 30 minutes, turn off heat and let chicken remain in water 20 minutes more. Remove from water and let cool enough to handle. Pull meat from bones and shred into bite-size pieces.
2. Wash and dry lettuce. Shred crosswise in 1-inch strips. Arrange in shallow serving bowl or platter. Arrange chicken on top.
3. Mix soy sauce, vinegar, corn syrup, garlic and salt.
4. Heat peanut oil in small skillet. Add scallions, ginger and peppercorns and sauté just long enough to release flavor of ginger. Mix in chili and sesame oils. Remove from heat. Stir in soy sauce mix, immediately pour over chicken and serve.

Serves 4

COLD CURRIED CHICKEN

The English found that hot curry made India's hot climate more acceptable. They should have tried cold curry, like this.

1 whole chicken
1 rib celery, chopped
1 carrot, chopped
1 onion, chopped

Sauce

8 tablespoons butter
1 stalk celery, in 1-inch pieces
2 onions, in 1-inch wedges
1 tomato, chopped coarsely
1 potato, in 1-inch cubes
2 apples, in 1-inch cubes
2 stalks cilantro, chopped coarsely
¼ teaspoon dried thyme
¼ teaspoon marjoram
1 bay leaf
¼ cup raw rice
1 tablespoon curry powder
Salt and pepper
Juice of ½ lemon
1 cup mayonnaise
¼ cup minced cilantro

1. Poach room-temperature chicken, along with chopped celery, carrot and onion, in enough boiling water to submerge. Boil 30 minutes, turn off heat and let chicken remain in water 20 minutes more. Remove from water and let cool enough to handle. Pull meat from bones and shred into bite-size pieces. Chill.
2. Boil poaching liquid, chicken bones and vegetables to reduce until about 2 cups liquid remain. Strain, degrease and reserve for use in sauce below.
3. Prepare sauce by sautéing celery, onions, tomato, potato, apples, cilantro, thyme, marjoram, bay leaf and rice in butter over low heat 12-15 minutes, until tender. Add curry powder and 2 cups chicken stock (from poaching), and simmer about 1 hour, until thick.
4. Puree in processor or blender. Strain through fine sieve. Salt and pepper to taste. Stir in lemon juice. Chill.
5. When cold, stir in mayonnaise. Pour over chicken, mix, sprinkle with minced cilantro and serve.

Serves 4-6

CHICKEN IN ORANGE SAUCE

Here's an adaptation of a Caribbean favorite that was adapted from French cuisine. That's the way it goes in cookery.

1 whole chicken, cut up
2 tablespoons flour
Salt and pepper
4 tablespoons vegetable oil
2 tablespoons sherry
1½ cups orange juice
2 tablespoons white wine vinegar
1 tablespoon brown sugar
2 cloves garlic, minced
1 teaspoon minced fresh basil (or ½ teaspoon dried)
2 oranges, peeled and sectioned

1. Dredge chicken pieces in mixture of flour, salt and pepper. Brown chicken in oil. Remove chicken to covered casserole or baking pan.
2. Pour off oil from skillet. Deglaze pan with sherry over high heat, scraping up brown bits and adding them to casserole.
3. Add all ingredients except orange sections to casserole. Bring to boil on stove, reduce heat to low, cover and simmer gently 40-45 minutes, until chicken is nearly done and sauce is thickened.
4. Add orange slices, re-cover and simmer 5 minutes more. Serve hot.

Serves 4-6

Cold
Curried
Chicken

Chicken in
Orange
Sauce

Tea-Smoked
Chicken

Baked
Chicken
with
Cranberry
Marinade

TEA-SMOKED CHICKEN

This Chinese preparation is not as difficult as it might appear. All it requires is a wok, a couple of ingredients not common to American kitchens and patience.

 1 *whole chicken*
 2 *teaspoons salt*
 4 *slices fresh ginger*
 1 *scallion, cut into pieces*
 1 *tablespoon sherry*
 1 *tablespoon soy sauce*
 2 *tablespoons black tea*
 2 *tablespoons brown sugar*
 2 *tablespoons uncooked white rice*

Sauce

 3 *tablespoons light soy sauce*
 2 *tablespoons red wine vinegar*
 1 *tablespoon sesame oil*
 2 *teaspoons Asian garlic-chili paste*
 2 *tablespoons sugar*

1. Rub chicken with salt inside and out. Scatter ginger and scallion along with sherry in cavity. Steam in large covered pot on rack, or in steamer, 40 minutes. Cool completely and rub with soy sauce.
2. Line wok, including cover, with foil. Mix tea, sugar and rice and mound on bottom of wok. Place chicken on its back on greased rack above mound. Turn heat to high. When mound begins to smoke, cover wok tightly and smoke 5 minutes. Turn chicken onto breast and smoke 10 minutes more. Cut chicken into small pieces and cool to room temperature.
3. To prepare sauce, blend all ingredients well. Serve with chicken pieces.
Serves 4-6

BAKED CHICKEN WITH CRANBERRY MARINADE

This winter dish can be transformed into a summer barbecue preparation as well. Directions for both are given.

 1 *whole chicken, cut up*
 ¼ *cup light soy sauce*
 3 *cloves garlic, sliced*
 ¼ *cup olive oil*
 1 *teaspoon minced fresh ginger*
 2 *tablespoons lemon juice*
 1 *teaspoon lemon pepper (or black pepper)*
 1½ *tablespoons sugar*
 ¼ *teaspoon salt*
 1 *tablespoon dry sherry*
 1 *cup cranberry sauce (see below)*

1. Combine all ingredients in glass dish and marinate chicken at room temperature 2 hours (or longer, in refrigerator). Turn pieces occasionally.

• As a Winter Dish:
2. To bake, arrange chicken pieces in a single layer in a large, buttered baking dish. Pour marinade over chicken and bake at 350°F for 1 hour, basting frequently.
3. Transfer chicken to serving dish. Cover and keep warm. Simmer pan juices to reduce slightly. Serve warm with chicken.

• As a Barbecue:
2. Remove chicken from marinade and grill or broil. Meanwhile, simmer marinade to reduce by about one-third and serve warm with chicken.
Serves 4-6

Cranberry Sauce

 1 *cup water*
 1 *cup sugar*
 2 *cups cranberries*

 Boil water and sugar 5 minutes. Add cranberries, reduce heat and simmer 5 minutes. Puree in processor or blender. (You'll need 1 cup.)

CHICKEN WITH BROCCOLI

Quick but elegant, this is the kind of dish cooks need when guests arrive unexpectedly.

 4 whole chicken breasts, halved
    and boned
 4 tablespoons brandy
 3 bunches broccoli (about 4 pounds)
    Salt and pepper
10 tablespoons butter
 2 tablespoons vegetable oil
½ cup dry vermouth
 8 tablespoons flour
 4 cups chicken stock
 1 cup cream, whipped to soft peaks
⅔ cup grated Parmesan

1. Brush chicken breasts with brandy on both sides and let them marinate for 15 minutes.
2. Peel main broccoli stalks and cut off to within 3 inches of flowerets. Blanch in boiling salted water 5 minutes. Drain immediately and plunge in cold water to cool. Drain again.
3. Salt and pepper chicken breasts lightly and sauté in 2 tablespoons of the butter and the oil 2 minutes on one side and 2 minutes on the other. Remove from pan and reserve. Deglaze pan with vermouth, letting most of it evaporate. Reserve liquid.
4. Melt remaining butter in saucepan over medium-low heat. Stir in flour and cook, stirring, until it begins to color. Add chicken stock. Stirring constantly, bring to boil and simmer for 5 minutes. Remove from heat. Gently stir in whipped cream and half the Parmesan.
5. Arrange broccoli in one layer in large buttered baking dish, with flowerets facing outward. Spoon half the sauce over the broccoli. Place chicken breasts, slightly overlapping, on broccoli stalks in middle of dish. Pour remaining sauce over chicken. Sprinkle with remaining Parmesan.
6. Bake at 350°F for about 25 minutes, until sauce bubbles on sides. Brown under broiler. Serve immediately.

Serves 6-8

CHICKEN WITH GIN AND MUSHROOMS

Sounds odd, tastes terrific.

 1 pound domestic mushrooms
 4 tablespoons butter
    Lemon juice
 1 whole chicken, cut up
 2 tablespoons vegetable oil
    Salt and pepper
¼ cup gin
 1 cup chicken stock
 1 cup cream
 1 teaspoon red currant jelly

1. Trim mushroom stems close to caps. Leave whole if small, slice if large. Sauté in 2 tablespoons of the butter over high heat until moisture has evaporated. Splash with lemon juice, stir and cook 1 minute more. Remove and reserve.
2. Pat chicken dry. Add remaining butter and vegetable oil to skillet and brown chicken over medium-high heat. Salt and pepper to taste. Turn off heat and remove excess fat.
3. Warm gin in small pan, pour over chicken and flame. Add chicken stock, bring to boil, cover and simmer over low heat until chicken is tender, about 30 minutes. (White meat should finish sooner.) Remove chicken to warm platter.
4. Reduce pan juices by boiling 5 minutes. Add cream and jelly and cook until the sauce begins to thicken. Add mushrooms and heat through. Pour over chicken and serve immediately.

Serves 4

Chicken
with
Preserved
Lemons

Baked
Chicken
Breasts with
Apricots

CHICKEN WITH PRESERVED LEMONS

One of the most famous of Moroccan dishes, this requires preserved lemons, which are hard to find in this country. If you're willing to make your own, however, the rewards will be substantial. Ben Alaoui of the Mamounia restaurant in Seattle preserves lemons and prepares the dish this way.

>   2 whole chickens, trimmed of fat and
>   skin
>   5 medium onions, minced
>   2 bunches parsley, chopped finely
>   1/2 clove garlic, chopped finely
>   7 tablespoons olive oil
>   1/4 pound butter
>   1 teaspoon coriander seeds
>   1 teaspoon ground ginger
>   1 teaspoon stem saffron
>   1 teaspoon pepper
>   1 teaspoon salt
>   4 quartered preserved lemons (see below)

1. Place chickens on their sides in casserole or deep baking pan. Combine onions, parsley, and garlic with olive oil, butter and spices. Pour over chickens. Add water to reach halfway up chickens. Bake at 350°F for about 45 minutes, until chickens are tender, turning halfway through.
2. Remove chickens and reserve in warm oven. Over high heat on stove, reduce sauce until it's thick, about 5 minutes. Arrange chickens and lemons on platter, pour sauce over them and serve.

Serves 6-8

Preserved Lemons

Quarter lemons to within 1/2 inch of bottoms so they don't completely separate. Sprinkle exposed flesh generously with coarse salt and press lemons back together in original shape. Sprinkle bottom of glass jar or stoneware crock with 1 tablespoon salt and fill with lemons, compacting them tightly. Cover tightly and leave at room temperature for 2 weeks. Before using, rinse lemons under cold water and discard juice in jar.

BAKED CHICKEN BREASTS WITH APRICOTS

Nina Lyman, a Spokane caterer, created this dish when she once had an apricot tree in her backyard. She serves it with rice.

>   4 chicken breast halves
>   Flour
>   Salt and pepper
>   1/4 cup clarified butter
> 1 1/2 cups peeled, pitted apricot halves
>   1/2 cup raisins
>   1/4 teaspoon cinnamon
>   1/8 teaspoon ground cloves
>   8 small new potatoes
>   1/2 cup chicken stock

1. Shake chicken breasts in bag containing flour and salt and pepper to taste. Shake excess flour off breasts. In heavy casserole, brown breasts in clarified butter over medium heat.
2. Combine apricots, raisins, cinnamon and cloves. Pour over chicken breasts. Surround chicken with new potatoes. Pour chicken stock in casserole, cover and bake at 350°F for 20 minutes. Uncover and bake 10 minutes more.

Serves 4

CRAB

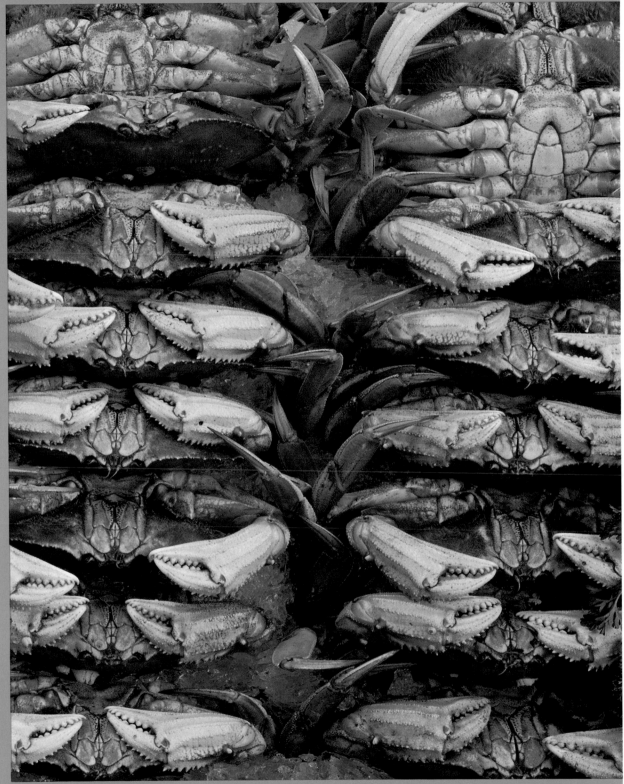

CRAB

In a properly ordered world, there would be no turkeys on winter holiday tables in Washington. Instead of with a bird, Washingtonians would celebrate with a crustacean, the Dungeness crab. For winter is when Dungeness crabs, in availability and quality, reach their peak, and no crab anywhere matches them.

That statement will outrage partisans of, say, Chesapeake Bay blue crabs or Florida stone crabs. Sorry, but it's true. In fact, by comparison lesser crabs are so thinly flavored they need spices and condiments and even deep-frying to make them appealing.

The Dungeness crab, on the other hand, stands on its own. Its full, sweet flavor is best savored right from the shell with no accompaniment at all. Oh, perhaps a touch of lemon juice or clarified butter might be nice, but nothing more.

Dungeness crabs are not Washington's alone. They're trapped commercially from Alaska's Aleutian Islands south to San Francisco. Their name, however, comes from a spot on the Olympic Peninsula, an indication of how closely Washington is identified with this famous delicacy.

To be precise, Dungeness is the name of a town on the English Channel. The name was transported here by Captain George Vancouver in 1792 when he was exploring the Strait of Juan de Fuca and came across an area near a long, curving sand spit that reminded him of a place called Dungeness in his native England.

A fishing village eventually was established near the spit, and the settlement's first commercial fishery was for the large, gray-brown, purple-tinged crabs that became known by the village's name. From there, the Dungeness crab's fame spread throughout the world, wherever crab fanciers are found.

In Washington, Dungeness crabs can be purchased nearly year-round. The coastal season runs from December 1 to September 15 and the Puget Sound season from October 1 to April 15. Often, however, crabs available in Washington markets actually are from Alaska. This is because Dungeness crabs are not reliable. Sometimes they're not of a good quality. Sometimes they're few in number.

The Dungeness crab fishery is a cyclical business. Some years Washington commercial crabbers land 18 or 19 million pounds. Some years the catch plummets to a paltry 4 million pounds. The reason for the fluctuation is something of a mystery. What is known is that Dungeness crabs seem to operate on a 10-year cycle.

Most biologists believe the crabs themselves are largely responsible for the cycle. Dungeness crabs are cannibalistic. When many young crabs are available, the adult crabs feast. It takes no special insight to see

CRAB CANNELLONI

Serve as a generous first course or the warm centerpiece of a buffet.

Filling

>2 tablespoons butter
>3 tablespoons minced shallots or scallions
>1½ cups crab meat, flaked
>Salt and pepper
>¼ cup dry vermouth

Melt butter in skillet, stir in shallots or scallions and saute over moderate heat for one minute. Add crab and warm through. Salt and pepper. Add vermouth and boil rapidly until it's nearly evaporated. Set filling aside in bowl.

Sauce

>⅓ cup dry vermouth
>2 tablespoons cornstarch
>2 tablespoons milk
>1½ cups cream
>¼ teaspoon salt
>White pepper
>½ cup grated Fontina cheese

In skillet, boil vermouth rapidly until reduced to a tablespoon. Remove from heat. Blend cornstarch and milk, then add to skillet along with cream, salt and white pepper to taste. Simmer for 2 minutes. Blend in cheese and simmer for 30 seconds. (Add more milk if sauce is too thick.)

Pasta

>2 cups unbleached flour
>2 large eggs
>2 teaspoons olive oil
>Salt

1. Mound flour on board. Make well in middle of mound and break eggs into well. Add oil and salt. Mix well with fork, then incorporate flour little by little from lower part of inner ring. When half the flour is absorbed, switch to hands and begin kneading until almost all flour is absorbed.
2. If using pasta machine, follow instructions and roll out sheet as thin as possible. If rolling out by hand, knead dough 10 minutes, then roll out as thin as possible with pin on floured board into single sheet. Let pasta dry 10 minutes.
3. Cut pasta into 6-inch squares. Cook one by one in large amount of boiling salted water, cooking each for only a few seconds until it rises to top of boiling water.
4. Transfer cooked pasta squares to bowl of cold water to which 2 tablespoons of olive oil have been added. Cool pasta squares and place on dampened cotton towels for about 20 minutes.

Assembly

>¼ cup grated Parmesan
>2 tablespoons butter

1. Lightly butter baking dish. Blend half of sauce with crab mixture.
2. Place generous spoonful of crab mixture on lower third of each pasta square, then roll into cylinder. Arrange cylinders closely together in baking dish, spoon over remainder of sauce, sprinkle with Parmesan and dot with 2 tablespoons of butter.
3. Bake at 425°F for 15-20 minutes, until bubbling hot and slightly browned. Serve immediately.

Serves 6 to 8

Note: Crepes can be substituted for cannelloni shells. Specialty food stores often carry both frozen crepes and cannelloni shells, if you prefer.

Louis Summers of Westport trapping a crab.

how this affects future generations. At some point, though, the ratio between old and young reaches a turning point, and the cycle will swing up again. Then it's Washingtonians who feast.

No matter where the crab cycle stands at any given time, certain fundamentals about buying and cooking Dungeness crab remain constant. The first is that Dungeness crab never is better than when it has just come from the sea. A live crab fresh from its hab-

itat is in the ideal state for plunking into a pot of boiling water. Short of those circumstances, all crab buying, cooking and eating involve some compromise.

Buying crabs kept alive in water tanks ranks second. Some fanciers contend that crabs become mushy in live tanks; certainly long residence in a tank does nothing to enhance a crab's flavor and texture. Live tanks are not common, unfortunately. Most people must buy cooked crabs that are sold

CRAB SOUFFLÉ

Here's a way to get the most out of a moderate amount of leftover crab. Bring this to your holiday table as an appetizer or serve as part of a hot buffet. Spurning the usual soufflé dish and baking it on a platter or in a Pyrex dish means the soufflé will expose more surface for browning and will be that much more inviting.

  6 tablespoons butter
  5 tablespoons flour
  ½ cup cream
  1 cup clam juice
    Salt and pepper
  8 tablespoons grated Parmesan
  5 large eggs, separated
  ¼ teaspoon dry mustard
  1 teaspoon lemon juice
  4 drops Tabasco
  ½ pound crab meat, flaked

1. In small, heavy-bottomed pan, melt butter, add flour and cook 5-7 minutes, stirring continuously.
2. Combine cream and clam juice and scald. Remove roux from heat and add scalded cream mixture all at once. Stir until blended and return to heat, turning up to medium. Stirring continuously, simmer until thick and smooth. Continue cooking another 5 minutes. Salt and pepper to taste and add 4 tablespoons of the cheese.
3. Let cool slightly and add egg yolks one at a time, stirring briskly after each. Add mustard, lemon juice and Tabasco. Fold in crab meat.
4. Generously butter oven-proof platter about 13 inches by 9 inches or Pyrex dish of same size. Sprinkle butter with 2 tablespoons of the cheese.
5. Beat egg whites until stiff but not dry. Fold gently into crab-cream mixture. Pour onto platter and sprinkle top with remaining cheese.
6. Bake at 450°F on top shelf 10-12 minutes. Top should be well browned and middle creamy but not runny. Serve immediately.

Serves 8-10

CRAB STEW

On a cold winter evening, with crusty fresh bread and a green salad, this stew will warm the soul as well as the ribs.

  3 tablespoons butter
  1 clove garlic, chopped
  3 scallions, sliced
  2 tablespoons flour
  1 large tomato or 1 cup canned tomato
  1 cup chicken stock
  1 cup cream
  1 pound crab meat
  ½ cup sherry
    Salt and pepper
  4 croutons (see note below)

1. Melt butter in soup pot. Lightly brown garlic in butter and discard. Add scallions and sauté 2 minutes. Add flour and cook, stirring, 5 minutes.
2. Puree fresh tomato in food mill (or drain, puree and strain canned tomato). Add tomato pulp, chicken stock and cream to pot. Bring to boil, stirring, and simmer 5 minutes, until taste of flour is gone.
3. Add crab and sherry. Salt and pepper to taste. Serve immediately with croutons and, if available, a sprinkle of chopped fresh dill.

Serves 4

Note: *To make croutons, slice French or Italian bread, butter slices (or dribble with olive oil) and toast them in a 325°F oven until lightly browned.*

fresh or frozen. Buying crabs in either of those states is risky, unless one knows a reliable fishmonger.

Start by ascertaining whether a crab has been frozen. If it has, it's likely to be tough and stringy, although some handling-and-freezing processes are better than others. Here, you have to rely on your basic fishmonger's knowledge.

When buying cooked, unfrozen crab, start by sniffing it. There should be no pronounced fishy odor. Then make certain a crab has a hard shell. Crabs molt, moving out of their shells and growing larger ones. The soft-shell stage of a Dungeness crab, unlike some other types, is not desirable.

Next, heft the crab. If it seems heavy for its size, it's most likely a good crab, for it has fully grown into its new quarters. Some crabs have barnacles on their shells. That, too, is a good sign, for it indicates a crab has lived in its shell a long time and will have grown into it.

Cooking Dungeness crabs is a simple process. Plunge them alive into a large amount of salted, boiling water (2 tablespoons salt per quart). When the water returns to a boil, cook for about 20 minutes. Timing can vary, depending on the size of the crabs and the amount of water. One commercial crabber's wife known for her cooking uses a four-gallon pot and cooks crab for precisely 19 minutes.

If you prefer to clean crabs before cooking, pry off the shells, break the crabs in half, shake out the viscera, pluck out the gills and drop into boiling water immediately. Cut back the salt to 1 tablespoon per quart of water and cook 12 to 15 minutes. Do not cook crabs that have been dead more than a couple of hours.

To most tastes, Dungeness crab is best when chilled. If that's your preference, plunge crabs directly from the pot into ice water to stop them from cooking further and prevent mushiness. After a crab has cooled in the ice water, it can be cracked and eaten or kept for a day in the refrigerator.

Two tips passed along from the crab fisherman's wife: she adds 1/4 cup of vegetable oil to her pot to keep it from boiling over; and she swears that sprinkling 1/4 cup of fresh or dried celery leaves into the boiling water before the crabs go in keeps odor out of the house. It's worth a try.

BAKED TIGER PRAWNS STUFFED WITH CRAB

Michele and Norbert Juhasz, natives of Lyon, France, migrated to Washington via California and opened the splendid restaurant, C'est Si Bon, just east of Port Angeles. Michele created this dish as a tribute to Dungeness crab.

12-16 tiger prawns, shelled
½ pound crab meat
¼ teaspoon lemon zest
Salt and pepper
Pinch cayenne
4 tablespoons clarified butter

Sauce

¾ cup fish stock or clam juice
¾ cup cream
¼ cup sherry
¼ teaspoon lemon zest
Salt and pepper
Pinch cayenne

1. Butterfly prawns by splitting length-wise down middle almost all the way through and spreading open. Lay them cut side up in buttered baking pan.
2. Sauté crab meat with lemon zest, salt and pepper to taste and cayenne in clarified butter for about 30 seconds. Immediately remove from heat and divide mixture among prawns, spooning it into cavities.
3. Cover stuffed prawns with waxed paper or buttered parchment. Bake at 450°F for about 10 minutes, until prawns lose their transparency.
4. Meanwhile, prepare sauce by combining fish stock or clam juice and cream and boiling to reduce by nearly two-thirds. Add sherry and lemon zest and reduce a bit more. Salt and pepper to taste and add cayenne.
5. Serve stuffed prawns immediately, spooning sauce over them and gar-nishing with lemon slices and parsley.

Serves 4

CRAB SCRAMBLE

For breakfast, lunch or light supper, this Chinese-style scrambled egg dish is as aromatic as it is savory.

½ pound crab meat, flaked
4 eggs
1 cup chicken stock
2 tablespoons light soy sauce
5 tablespoons vegetable oil
1 tablespoon minced fresh ginger
1 scallion, chopped finely
1 tablespoon cornstarch
2 tablespoons water
1 tablespoon red wine vinegar

1. Combine crab, eggs, chicken stock and soy sauce. Beat lightly.
2. Sauté ginger and scallion over medium-high heat in 1 tablespoon of the vegetable oil for 30-40 seconds. Remove and reserve.
3. Add 3 tablespoons vegetable oil to skillet along with crab-egg mixture. Cook, stirring slowly for a few seconds. Add ginger and scallion while stirring. Cook about 2 minutes while scrambling eggs. Mix cornstarch with water to make paste, then stir paste into eggs to thicken. Stir in vinegar and final tablespoon oil. Serve immediately.

Serves 2-4

BROILED CRAB VINAIGRETTE

Appetizer or first course, this requires time to marinate but little time to prepare.

>   1 pound crab meat, cooled
>   ¼ cup olive oil
>   2 tablespoons white wine vinegar
>   1 tablespoon capers, rinsed and drained
>   1 tablespoon minced scallion
>   1 tablespoon minced fresh dill
>   1 tablespoon minced parsley
>   Salt ·
>   Lemon pepper (or black pepper)
>   Mayonnaise
>   Parmesan, grated

1. Combine crab with all ingredients except mayonnaise and Parmesan. Salt and pepper to taste. Chill several hours or overnight.
2. Stir 2 tablespoons mayonnaise into mixture. Divide mixture among scallop shells or toast rounds. Spread a little mayonnaise over each. Sprinkle with Parmesan. Broil until just browned. Serve immediately.

Serves 6-8

CRAB BUTTER

Here's a method of extracting flavor from crab shells. Use the butter to top grilled fish or flavor sauces and soups.

>   2 tablespoons butter
>   1 onion, chopped coarsely
>   1 celery stalk, chopped coarsely
>   1 carrot, chopped coarsely
>   1 clove garlic, minced
>   1 bay leaf
>   ¼ teaspoon dried thyme
>   ¼ teaspoon dried tarragon
>   Shells of 2-3 crabs
>   3 tablespoons brandy
>   3 pounds unsalted butter
>   ¼ cup tomato sauce

1. Sauté onion, celery, carrot, garlic, bay leaf, thyme and tarragon in 2 tablespoons butter over medium heat 3-4 minutes. Add crab shells and brandy and cook, stirring, 3 more minutes. Add 3 pounds butter and tomato sauce, cover and barely simmer about 2 hours.
2. Strain through sieve, pressing juice from solids. Let stand 15-20 minutes, skim froth and strain through dampened layers of cheesecloth, leaving residue in pan. Cool and refrigerate or freeze.

Makes about 6 cups

SAUCES FOR CRACKED CRAB

Though cold Dungeness crab in its shell seems best with as little adornment as possible, some people prefer their crab with a sauce. Here are three choices.

Bagna Cauda

"Hot bath" in Italian, this variation on a classic dip for cold vegetables goes nicely with crab, too. For a party, keep the bagna cauda bubbling in a fondue pot or chafing dish in the middle of the table. Spoon some of the sauce into containers for the crab and have guests dip vegetables (such as strips of pepper, jicama, carrot and cucumber as well as celery and scallions) in the central pot. Have bread sticks or chunks of crusty bread available for dipping, also.

> 4 cups cream
> 8 tablespoons butter
> 16 anchovy fillets, chopped finely
> 4 teaspoons chopped garlic

1. Simmer cream to reduce by half by boiling until it's thick and then continue to simmer briskly.
2. Melt the butter over low heat. Add anchovies and garlic. Stir, add cream, turn up heat to medium and bring nearly to boiling point. Serve hot.

Serves 4

Aioli

Here's another variation on a classic sauce, this one French.

> 1 tablespoon dried bread crumbs
> 1 tablespoon red wine vinegar
> 2 tablespoons lemon juice
> 6 cloves garlic, chopped
> 2 egg yolks
> 1 teaspoon Dijon-style mustard
>   Salt and white pepper
> ½ cup olive oil
> ½ cup peanut oil

1. Moisten bread crumbs with vinegar. Puree bread crumbs, lemon juice, garlic, egg yolks and mustard in a processor or blender. Salt and pepper to taste.
2. With the processor or blender running, add oils in a steady stream, very slowly at first, until the sauce becomes thick and shiny. Chill. Serve cold.

Serves 4

Chili-Tomato Sauce

This is the simplest of the sauces, and the most traditional—a sort of "cocktail" sauce.

> 1 cup mayonnaise
> 1 tablespoon chili sauce
> ¼ teaspoon Worcestershire sauce
> 1 tomato, peeled, seeded and chopped
> 1 tablespoon minced parsley

Combine all ingredients thoroughly. Chill and serve cold.

Serves 4

CRAB MOUSSE

Though her husband, Angelo Pellegrini, has the reputation as a food, wine and gardening authority, friends of Seattle's Virginia Pellegrini know her as an outstanding cook in her own right. Here's a favorite dish that she serves as an appetizer or as part of a buffet.

> 1 can mushroom soup
> 6 ounces cream cheese, at room temperature
> 1 envelope unflavored gelatin
> 1 pound crab meat, flaked
> 1 cup chopped celery
> ¼ cup chopped scallion
> ¾ cup mayonnaise
> Juice of half a lemon
> Tabasco
> Seasoning salt

1. Melt soup and cream cheese together in pan over medium heat, stir in gelatin and set aside to cool slightly.
2. Mix other ingredients, add a few drops of Tabasco if desired and season mixture to taste.
3. Mix together all ingredients, pour into lightly greased mold and chill thoroughly. Serve with bread, toast rounds or crackers.

Serves 10-12

STEAMED CRAB DUMPLINGS

These little savories require small cups as cooking vessels. Use sake cups or a child's teacups, or fashion your own. For the latter, take the cap from a condiment bottle and use it to mold cups from foil. Serve the dumplings as an appetizer or with a multi-course Chinese meal.

> ½ pound crab meat, chopped finely
> ¼ pound ground pork
> 2 tablespoons finely chopped fresh coriander
> ¼ teaspoon pepper
> 5 cloves garlic, minced
> 1 tablespoon finely chopped scallion
> 2 tablespoons Chinese oyster sauce
> 1 teaspoon sesame oil
> 1 tablespoon soy sauce
> 1 egg
> 1 egg yolk, lightly beaten

Mix all ingredients except egg yolk. Fill cups with mixture, brush with egg yolk and steam on rack in covered container 20 minutes. Serve immediately or at room temperature with soy sauce. Serves 4-6

CRAB PATÉ

This is an easy dish to prepare, and the crab flavor is not submerged.

> 8 ounces cream cheese, at room temperature
> 8 tablespoons butter, at room temperature
> ¼ cup chopped onion
> 1 cup crab meat, flaked
> 2 tablespoons lemon juice
> 1 teaspoon lemon pepper
> 1 teaspoon salt
> 2 teaspoons curry powder

1. Using a food processor, combine cream cheese, butter and onion. Process 2-3 minutes until smooth (or beat well by hand).
2. Add crab and other ingredients and process another 1-2 minutes until smooth. Adjust seasoning. Transfer to serving bowl and cover with plastic wrap. Refrigerate at least 3 hours. Serve chilled with crackers or bread rounds.

Serves 8-10

MUSHROOMS

MUSHROOMS

Of all the gastronomic bounty flourishing in Washington, perhaps the most precious—literally as well as figuratively—is the wealth of wild mushrooms. Many Washingtonians have only recently discovered this treasure. First- and second-generation immigrants from Europe and Asia know that Washington's forests and meadows yield dozens of varieties of edible mushrooms. But for Washingtonians cut off from the culinary knowledge of their forebears, the presence and value of these mushrooms was a secret until the wave of "ethnic" cooking swept America.

Now, certain wild mushrooms have become important cash crops in Washington, and they frequently can be found in markets among the cabbages and celery.

Veteran mushroom hunters worry about the boom in popularity. They say that commercial pickers, not to mention the increased number of amateurs, might be overpicking. To the veteran hunters, mushrooms are not only a culinary resource but also an important part of Washington's recreational lifestyle.

Mushroom stalkers experience more than just the flavor of their prey. They enjoy the thrill of the hunt, the exhilaration of a tromp in the outdoors and the companionship of friends. The friends must be close, however, for no mushroom

hunter (except certain generous members of the various mycological societies who conduct expeditions for novices) readily shares the secrets of his hunting ground.

A mushroom is, unglamorously, a fungus. Much about fungi still baffles scientists, partly accounting for the aura of mystery surrounding wild mushrooms. Though many attempts have been made, few varieties can be cultivated. The most common exception, *Agaricus bisporus*, is the white "button" mushroom seen in grocery stores. Shiitake, the golden-to-deep-brown umbrella-shaped mushrooms, and creamy fan-shaped oyster mushrooms are other notable exceptions. Most varieties, however, stubbornly resist being tamed, and their rarity only increases their desirability.

Perhaps 50 types of Washington's wild mushrooms are edible, 20 or so of which are considered choice. Listing them all is the function of a field guide, not of this book. Fortunately, a number of excellent field guides are available in bookstores and libraries. They contain descriptions, photographs and drawings and warnings about those mushrooms to steer clear of. If you're new at mushroom hunting, remember the mushroom hunter's fundamental rule: When in doubt, throw it out.

Certain wild mushrooms are more important in the kitchen than others, partly

BEGGAR'S MUSHROOMS

Tidy little bundles of dough stuffed with wild mushrooms; this dish makes a dramatic first course or an attractive hot lunch.

  8 tablespoons butter
  4 shallots, minced
  4 cloves garlic, minced
  2 tablespoons chopped parsley
  2 pounds fresh morels or boletes,
      sliced thickly
  ½ cup white wine
  ½ cup chicken or meat stock
  ½ cup crème fraiche (see Notes on Ingre-
      dients, page xi)
    Salt and pepper
    Melted butter
  ½ cup grated Parmesan
  8 10-inch crepes (see below)

1. Sauté shallots, garlic and parsley in butter for 5 minutes, until garlic turns light brown. Add mushrooms, raise heat and cook, stirring, until mushrooms give up their liquid and it has evaporated. Set mushrooms aside.
2. Add wine and let it evaporate. Add stock. Simmer 5 minutes as juices thicken. Add crème fraiche and salt and pepper to taste. Set aside to cool.
3. Place about ¼ cup mushroom mixture and a little sauce in the middle of each crepe. Cut a 12-inch-long strip of foil about ½ inch wide and fold strip over to double thickness. Pull up edges of pancake to form bag containing mushrooms and tie into bundle with foil strip. Place each bundle in buttered baking dish. (Bundles can be refrigerated at this point for 8-10 hours.) Dribble melted butter and sprinkle Parmesan over each bundle. Bake at 375°F for 10-12 minutes and serve hot.

Serves 8

Crepes

  4 eggs
  1 cup milk
1¼ cups flour
  ¼ cup water
  ½ teaspoon salt
  3 tablespoons melted butter, cooled

1. Mix all ingredients except butter in processor or blender. Stir in butter. Thin batter with milk if necessary to consistency of heavy cream.
2. Brush 7-inch skillet with some of a mixture of 3 tablespoons melted butter and 1 tablespoon vegetable oil. Place on medium-high heat. When hot, add about 3 tablespoons of the batter and swirl quickly to coat skillet. Cook until light gold, about 1 minute, flip and cook 30 seconds more. Cool on rack. (Stack between sheets of waxed paper and cover with plastic wrap if not using right away.)

Serves 8

Buying chanterelles at Olympia.

because of their flavor and partly because of their availability in markets. In no particular order, they are:

Chanterelle—This is the prey of most commercial mushroom pickers in Washington. Thousands of pounds are exported annually to Europe. (The French call chanterelles *girolles* and prize them highly. Germans call them *pfifferlinge* and esteem them just as highly.) Chanterelles are beautiful in form and color. They're shaped like curving trumpets and have delicate ribs. The most common color is a golden apricot, though some white chan-

terelles show up, too. Of all the wild mushrooms that can't be cultivated, chanterelles are the most commonly available in markets.

Boletus edulis—Of the several varieties of boletes (or close cousins) growing in Washington, the *Boletus edulis* unquestionably is king. Known as *cepes* in France and *porcini* (piglets) in Italy, *Boletes edulis* are firm, meaty mushrooms with bulbous stems and thick caps under which are dense arrays of tubes rather than the gills of meadow mushrooms. In size, boletes range from golf ball to toadstool and in color from

MUSHROOM SAUCE FOR PASTA

This combines dried boletes, or *porcini*, with fresh wild mushrooms, perhaps boletes again, or chanterelles or morels. It is a robust sauce so it should be served with a thicker cut of pasta: penne, for instance, or rigatoni, perhaps.

    2 ounces dried porcini
    2 cups warm water
    1 small onion, chopped finely
    1 clove garlic, minced
    1 cup finely chopped parsley
    4 tablespoons olive oil
    4 tablespoons butter
    1 pound wild mushrooms, sliced
    3 mild Italian sausages,
        casings removed
    3 tablespoons tomato paste
    2 cups beef stock
      Salt and pepper
 1½ pounds pasta
      Grated Parmesan

1. Soak dried mushrooms in warm water 20-30 minutes. Drain. Chop finely.
2. Sauté onion, garlic and parsley in 2 tablespoons of the olive oil and the butter over medium heat 10 minutes. Add fresh mushrooms and sauté about 15 minutes, until their liquid has evaporated. Mix in drained dried mushrooms. Remove from skillet and reserve.
3. In same skillet, lightly brown sausage meat in remaining olive oil, breaking up with fork. Do not overcook. Remove most fat from skillet.
4. Dissolve tomato paste in ½ cup of the beef stock. Add to sausage meat and cook 5 minutes. Add mushrooms and another ½ cup stock. Salt and pepper to taste. Reduce heat and simmer 30 minutes, adding stock as needed.
5. Cook pasta in boiling salted water. Drain, toss with sauce and serve immediately with grated Parmesan.

Serves 4-6

CREAM OF MUSHROOM SOUP

For non-mushroom hunters, here's a dish that combines domesticated button mushrooms with dried wild boletes, or *porcini*.

 1½ cups loosely packed dried porcini
    1 medium onion, finely chopped
    8 tablespoons butter
 1½ pounds button mushrooms, sliced
    ¼ cup flour
    6 cups chicken stock, heated
    2 egg yolks
    2 cups cream
      Salt and pepper

1. Soak *porcini* in 2 cups warm water for 30 minutes. Drain. (Strain and refrigerate liquid for use in dark-colored sauce or soup.) Rinse *porcini* and pat dry. Chop coarsely.
2. Sauté onion in butter over low heat for 10 minutes, but do not brown. Add button mushrooms and *porcini* to onion. Sauté gently until mushroom liquid has evaporated.
3. Sprinkle flour over mushrooms and stir until flour disappears. Pour in hot chicken stock and bring to boil while stirring. Cover, turn down heat and simmer 30 minutes.
4. Blend egg yolks with cream. Slowly add to soup and bring to boil. Salt and pepper to taste. Garnish with slices of button mushrooms and dollop of sour or whipped cream.

Serves 8

tan through red to deep brown. Boletes are particularly subject to despoiling by worms and insects. Since boletes are now appearing in markets, buyers should take care to avoid wormy or insect-ridden mushrooms unless, like some fanciers, they believe wildlife in mushrooms is rendered harmless by cooking.

Morel—Of the many morel varieties, two are likely to be encountered in Washington: black morels and white (or yellow) morels. There are also several kinds of so-called "false" morels that might be confused with the real thing by the uninitiated. Because of their pitted caps, which in shape and surface resemble certain pine cones, sometimes morels must be rinsed quickly to rid them of dirt. (In general, mushrooms should only be wiped with a damp cloth or scrubbed with a soft brush in order not to destroy flavor.)

Matsutake—In Japanese, *take* means mushroom. This mushroom, beloved by the Japanese, often grows under pine trees, *matsu.* Thus, it's sometimes called pine mushroom in this country. Firm, with a white flesh and a fairly flat cap that can grow up to 10 inches across, matsutake are frequently found in Asian markets during their fall season.

Oyster mushroom—With a taste and texture some people find to be reminiscent of oysters, this variety can be cultivated in decaying wood and thus is being grown commercially in Washington and sold fresh in markets.

Shiitake—Like oyster mushrooms, shiitake can be cultivated in wood and are grown commercially in Washington. That's the reason they're included in this article even though they don't grow wild in this state. Shiitake are the staple mushroom in Chinese and Japanese cooking, and dried shiitake imported from Asia are often sold in the United States as "Chinese" or "Japanese" mushrooms.

Mushrooms need rain to fruit. Their availability, then, can't easily be predicted beyond saying that more are available in Washington during the spring and fall than in other seasons. A wet summer on the Olympic Peninsula, where commercial picking for chanterelles is concentrated, means that chanterelles will be available in markets from June until late fall. Cultivated oyster mushrooms and shiitake, like button mushrooms, are usually sold fresh year-round.

Most mushrooms can be dried and reconstituted by soaking in warm water or other liquids. Delicately flavored varieties, however, lose much in the drying process. The flavor of some varieties, on the other hand, seems concentrated by drying. Boletes, for example, are splendid dried and are widely available in that form, usually under their Italian name, *porcini.* Dried chanterelles tend to be rubbery and are better preserved by sauteing and freezing.

Selecting wild mushrooms in the market can be tricky. Commercial pickers don't always handle mushrooms carefully. Look for dry, clean, plump mushrooms with no signs of wrinkling. When you get home from the market or woods, treat the mushrooms carefully. Some varieties have slippery skins. They should be peeled, but others shouldn't, even if, like some boletes, they seem slimy.

Fresh mushrooms may be stored for several days in the refrigerator, especially if they're not wet. If they are dry, lay them out in a single layer in a dish and cover with a damp cloth.

Some mushrooms mix well in cooking. Morels and boletes, for instance, make a good marriage. But delicately flavored varieties, such as oyster mushrooms, shouldn't be combined with stronger-flavored ones or they'll be overwhelmed.

Finally, when cooking mushrooms avoid aluminum, which may discolor them. Use stainless steel or enamel.

POLLO FORESTIERE

The name of this Italian dish is a tip-off: it's an earthy main course.

    3 tablespoons butter
    3 tablespoons olive oil
    1 whole chicken, cut into 12 pieces
      Salt and pepper
    2 tablespoons chopped shallots
    2 cloves garlic, minced
    1 tablespoon minced fresh rosemary (or
      1 teaspoon dried)
    1 pound chanterelles, sliced
    1 cup white wine
    2 tablespoons tomato paste
    1 cup canned tomatoes, drained
      and chopped
    2 cups chicken stock
    2 bay leaves

1. Melt butter combined with oil in large skillet. Brown chicken. Salt and pepper lightly, remove and set aside.
2. Add shallots, garlic and rosemary to skillet. Sauté 5 minutes. Add mushrooms, raise heat and cook until they give up their liquid and it has evaporated. Lower heat and add wine. Boil until wine is reduced by half.
3. Combine tomato paste and tomatoes. Add to mushrooms. Then add chicken stock and bay leaves. Partly cover and simmer for 30 minutes. Salt and pepper to taste.
4. Place chicken in skillet. Cut circle of foil to just fit in skillet. Place it on chicken, cover skillet with lid and simmer at lowest heat for 30 minutes, or until chicken is done.

Serves 4

Note: *This dish is better if cooled overnight and reheated. In that case, cook chicken only 20 minutes and finish cooking just before serving.*

MUSHROOMS IN PORT SAUCE

As a first course or an accompaniment to meat or poultry, this dish tastes deeply of the forest. Use either oyster mushrooms or chanterelles.

    2 tablespoons butter
    2 cloves garlic, minced
  ¼ cup chopped parsley
    1 pound fresh oyster mushrooms or
      chanterelles, sliced
 1½ tablespoons flour
  ½ cup strong chicken or meat stock
  ¼ cup Port
      Salt and pepper
    2 egg yolks
  ½ cup cream
    4 slices toast, crusts removed

1. Sauté garlic and parsley in butter over low heat 2 minutes. Add mushrooms and sauté 10-15 minutes, until their liquid has evaporated.
2. Sprinkle flour over mushrooms, add stock and Port and salt and pepper to taste. Cook, stirring, until sauce has reduced by half.
3. Beat egg yolks with cream. Stir into mushrooms and cook, stirring, until sauce thickens. Do not allow to boil.
4. Spoon mushrooms and sauce over toast and serve immediately.

Serves 4

MUSHROOM BRIOCHE LOAF

Any meaty wild mushrooms will do for this, but chanterelles seem to be best. Serve as an appetizer or snack. A couple of warm slices with mustard sauce (see page 7) makes a good first course.

Brioche Dough

½ tablespoon dry yeast
    Pinch sugar
2 tablespoons medium-hot tap water
2 eggs.
2 tablespoons milk
1¾ cups flour
1 teaspoon salt
6 tablespoons chilled unsalted butter,
    cut into bits

1. Dissolve yeast and sugar in water. Beat eggs and milk into yeast mixture. Stir in flour and salt. Knead on lightly floured surface into soft dough. Let rest 10 minutes. Knead butter into dough. Let rest 10 minutes. Knead 1 minute. Let rise 40 minutes in bowl covered with plastic wrap.
2. Turn out dough on lightly floured surface, pat down and fold twice. Pat down again. Fold again. Form into ball and let rise in bowl covered by plastic wrap until slightly more than doubled in bulk, about 2 hours.
3. In processor, make dough this way: Place flour and salt in processor bowl. Add chilled butter bits and process briefly until butter is broken into flour. Beat eggs and milk into yeast-sugar-water mixture. With processor running, add liquid until dough balls up. Turn out on lightly floured surface and let rest 10 minutes. Proceed as above with kneading and rising.

Mushroom Mixture

1 medium onion, minced
3 cloves garlic, minced
¼ cup minced parsley
2 tablespoons olive oil
2 tablespoons butter
1 tablespoon fresh thyme (or 1 teaspoon dried)
1 pound wild mushrooms,
    chopped coarsely
¼ cup dry vermouth
    Salt and pepper
½ cup minced prosciutto or boiled ham
⅓ cup pine nuts (optional)
1 cup grated Fontina, Swiss or
    Gruyère cheese
½ cup grated Parmesan
2 eggs, beaten

1. Sauté onion, garlic and parsley in butter and olive oil over medium heat 10 minutes. Add thyme and mushrooms and sauté about 15 minutes, until mushrooms' liquid has evaporated. Add vermouth and cook until it has evaporated. Salt and pepper to taste. Remove from heat, stir in prosciutto or ham and pine nuts. Cool mixture. Mix in cheeses and all but 2 tablespoons of the beaten eggs. Reserve remaining egg.
2. Pat down brioche dough after second rise and flour lightly. Pat into 10-by-14-inch rectangle. Place on baking sheet and refrigerate 10-15 minutes. Remove from refrigerator and place on lightly floured foil 18 inches wide and about 20 inches long.
3. Roll out dough to ¼-inch thickness. You should have a rectangle about 14 inches by 18 inches. Spread mushroom mixture on dough, leaving a 2-inch border all around. Using foil as aid, roll up dough lengthwise as you would a jellyroll.

4. Make wash by mixing remaining beaten egg with 1 teaspoon water. Use some wash to seal seam after pressing it together. Flip roll seam side down. Press end seams and fold under. Brush top with egg wash. (With leftover bits of dough, decorate roll with pastry shapes, if you wish.)

5. Bake on buttered baking sheet at 350°F about 55 minutes, until browned. Let rest 15-20 minutes before slicing and serving.

Serves 6-10

Note: *Try doubling recipe and making 2 loaves. If you want to reserve one for later use, bake it 20 minutes, let cool thoroughly, wrap in foil and freeze. When ready to use, thaw in refrigerator for at least 1 day, then bring to room · temperature, remove from foil and bake at 350°F 25-30 minutes.*

MARINATED MUSHROOMS

Chanterelles are ideal for this recipe, but other wild mushrooms will do, as well.

> 1 pound wild mushrooms, sliced
> 1 cup white wine
> 1½ cups olive oil
>   Tabasco
> 2 teaspoons salt
>   Pepper
> 3 tablespoons minced onion
> 3 cloves garlic, minced
> 1 lemon, sliced thinly
> 4 whole cloves
> 1 bay leaf
> 3 tablespoons minced parsley

1. Marinate mushrooms in wine for 45-60 minutes.
2. Whisk together olive oil, Tabasco to taste, salt and pepper to taste. Mix in onion, garlic, lemon slices, cloves and bay leaf.

3. Drain wine from mushrooms and add them to oil mixture. Toss gently. Store in jar or crock with tight-fitting lid and refrigerate 2-3 days before serving. Drain and sprinkle with parsley when served.

Serves 4-6

STIR-FRIED MUSHROOMS WITH CHINESE CABBAGE

Chinese cabbage, also known in this country as Nappa cabbage, is sweet and crisp. Here it's combined with shiitake, either dried or fresh, in a quick and simple vegetable dish.

> 6 fresh or dried shiitake
> 1 pound Chinese cabbage
>   Vegetable oil
> 4 ounces bamboo shoots, rinsed
>   and sliced
>   Salt

1. If using dried mushrooms, soak them in warm water at least 20 minutes and drain, reserving the soaking liquid.
2. Slice fresh or dried-and-soaked mushrooms thickly. Slice cabbage crosswise into thin strips.
3. Heat enough vegetable oil in wok or frying pan to just coat bottom. Stir-fry cabbage about 1 minute. Add mushrooms, bamboo shoots and salt to taste. Stir-fry 1 minute, add 2 tablespoons water (or mushroom soaking liquid), cover and cook 3-5 minutes. Serve immediately.

Serves 4

Marinated
Mushrooms

Stir-Fried
Mushrooms
with
Chinese
Cabbage

DUXELLES

Here's the basic method of preparing full-flavored wild mushrooms such as boletes, chanterelles and morels as a side dish or as an addition to sauces and soups. Duxelles may be frozen.

> 2 pounds wild mushrooms
> ¼ cup butter
> ¼ cup olive oil
> ½ cup minced shallots
> 3 cloves garlic, minced
> ¼ cup fresh tarragon (if not fresh, omit)
> 1½ teaspoons salt
> Pepper

1. Chop mushrooms coarsely. Heat butter and oil in large skillet over medium-high heat. Add shallots and garlic and sauté until pale gold, about 5 minutes. Add mushrooms and stir until well coated.
2. Cook, stirring occasionally, until mushrooms give up their liquid and it has evaporated. Add tarragon, salt and pepper and sauté over medium-low heat about 15 minutes. Cool before freezing.

Makes 3-4 cups

Note: When serving as a side dish to meat or fish, add a little cream in final moments of cooking.

PELLEGRINI'S MUSHROOM-RABBIT SAUCE

Dr. Angelo Pellegrini is an Emeritus Professor of English at the University of Washington; prolific author of books and essays on cooking, the kitchen garden, wine making, the immigrant's experience in America, and "living appropriately"; and a generous friend and tutor to the authors. He does not teach recipes so much as principles. Nevertheless, from observation comes this example of his kitchen mastery, a sauce of surpassing flavor. Appropriate for pasta or rice, here it's married to the ideal partner: the simple polenta of his Italian childhood.

> Dried porcini or morel mushrooms, or both
> 1 rabbit, cut up
> 2 tablespoons flour
> 2 tablespoons olive oil
> 1 pound Italian sausage, in 1-inch chunks
> 6 tablespoons lean salt pork, minced into paste
> ½ large onion, chopped finely
> 2 stalks celery, chopped finely
> 1 small carrot, chopped finely
> 3 cloves garlic, chopped finely
> ⅓ cup minced parsley
> 1 heaping cup sliced button mushrooms
> 1 heaping tablespoon capers, rinsed and drained
> 1½ teaspoons fresh thyme (or 1 teaspoon dried)
> 3 ounces tomato sauce
> 2-3 cups chicken or meat stock
> ¾ cup dry vermouth or white wine
> ¼ teaspoon nutmeg
> ¼ teaspoon allspice
> Peel of ½ lemon, minced
> Salt and pepper
> 1 teaspoon arrowroot
> Red pepper flakes or Tabasco (optional)

1. Soak dried mushrooms in warm water 20-30 minutes. Drain and chop coarsely (to make 1 cup), reserving ½ cup of the soaking liquid.
2. Cut most meat off rabbit thighs. Chop rest of rabbit into 1½-inch chunks. Pat dry. Sprinkle flour over chunks and brown them, including thigh bones, in olive oil, in heavy casserole. Remove rabbit from casserole and reserve.
3. Brown sausage chunks in same oil. Remove and reserve.
4. Add salt pork to oil in casserole and melt briefly. Add onion, celery, carrot, garlic and parsley. Cook over low heat 8-10 minutes. Add wild and button mushrooms, capers and thyme. Cook 5-8 minutes more. Mix tomato sauce with 2 cups stock, ½ cup of the mushroom liquid and vermouth or wine. Add to casserole and simmer 5 minutes. Add nutmeg, allspice, lemon peel and salt and pepper to taste. Sprinkle on arrowroot and stir well. Add red pepper flakes or Tabasco to taste, if desired.
5. Add rabbit and sausage. Add more stock if needed. (Liquid should come to within a couple of inches of the top of the meat.)
6. Bring to simmer on stove. Cook in 300°F oven 45 minutes to 1 hour. (Sauce can be cooled and refrigerated for a day or two or frozen.) Serve hot over polenta.

Serves 6-8

Polenta

Polenta, the simple food that sustained Italian peasants north of Rome for centuries, can be made thin or thick. Thin, it's ladled out of the pot like soft dumplings.

Thick, it should be of a consistency so that when its cooking pot is flipped quickly upside down on a board, it spreads only slightly before setting. Let it stand 30 minutes and slice off portions to be covered by the sauce.

Slices of thick, leftover polenta can be browned lightly on both sides under the broiler, buttered and served as an alternative to bread. Or brown them on both sides, then layer on slices of cheese—jack cheese is excellent—and melt the cheese under the broiler. Or saute slices in butter and serve them with syrup.

This recipe, for thick polenta, is not as elaborate as the other polenta recipe in this section. Both, however, require coarse-ground cornmeal to obtain the proper texture. This is often sold in specialty food stores under the simple label of polenta.

2 quarts water
2½ teaspoons salt
2¾ cups coarse-ground cornmeal

1. Bring water and salt to a boil. Stirring constantly, slowly add cornmeal in thin but steady stream.
2. Turn down heat to medium-low. Continue stirring, more or less constantly, 20-30 minutes, until polenta pulls away from sides of pan.
3. Flip pan upside down on wooden board, pulling pan away quickly so polenta spreads slightly.
4. Cool somewhat before spooning out or slicing portions to cover with sauce.

MUSHROOM POLENTA

Here's a somewhat elaborate version of polenta. Serve it either as a side dish or as a main course.

Mushroom Filling

1 pound chanterelle mushrooms
½ cup minced onion
2 cloves garlic, minced
2 tablespoons chopped parsley
2 tablespoons butter
1 tablespoon olive oil
¼ cup dry vermouth
   Salt and pepper

Polenta

1 cup chicken stock
1 cup coarse-ground cornmeal
2¼ cups boiling chicken stock
½ cup grated Gruyère cheese
¼ cup grated Parmesan
3 tablespoons sour cream
   Salt and pepper
1 tablespoon grated Parmesan
1 tablespoon butter, in bits

Bechamel Sauce

2 tablespoons butter
2 tablespoons flour
1 cup milk, scalded
   Salt

1. Prepare mushroom filling by slicing chanterelles, if they're small, or chopping coarsely, if they're large. Sauté onion, garlic and parsley in butter and oil over medium heat 10 minutes. Add mushrooms and sauté about 15 minutes, until their liquid has evaporated. Add vermouth and cook until it evaporates. Salt and pepper to taste.
2. In heavy pot, mix cold chicken stock with cornmeal. Place over medium heat and stir in boiling chicken stock. Bring to boil, reduce heat to low and cook 20 minutes, stirring frequently. Remove from heat and stir in Gruyère, ¼ cup Parmesan and sour cream. Salt and pepper to taste.

3. Prepare béchamel by melting butter in small pan over low heat. When it stops foaming, beat in flour and cook, stirring, 2 minutes without allowing to color. Remove from heat and pour in scalded milk all at once, beating to blend. Return pan to medium-high heat and, stirring, bring to boil. Then boil 2-3 minutes, stirring constantly. Salt to taste.
4. Pour half the polenta in deep, round, well-buttered 2-quart baking dish. Spread mushrooms over polenta. Top with remaining polenta. Spread béchamel on top. Sprinkle with 1 tablespoon Parmesan and dot with butter.
5. Bake at 350°F until bubbly, about 30 minutes. Serve hot.

Serves 6-8

MATSUTAKE WITH RICE

Here's a simple Japanese method of flavoring rice with the prized matsutake.

3 cups rice
5 cups water
5 tablespoons light soy sauce
5 tablespoons sake
⅓ pound fresh matsutake, sliced
   Salt

1. Wash rice and drain. Combine with water, soy sauce and sake in pan and bring to boil. Add mushrooms and salt to taste. Cover, reduce heat and simmer about 15 minutes, until water is absorbed and rice is tender.
2. Remove cover, raise heat and let steam 30 seconds. Serve immediately.

Serves 6

PEARS

At some point in the autumn, usually October, Washington food markets lay out an irresistible display of pears: bell-shaped Bartletts, egg-shaped Anjous, long-necked Boscs, little maroon Seckels, and crimson-freckled Forelles. For the pear fancier, this is the best time of year, bar none. Most of the pears come from Washington orchards, for Washington ranks as the nation's second-leading pear producer, growing nearly a third of the country's crop.

Like that of apples, Washington's pear production is centered in the Yakima and Wenatchee valleys. There the harvest begins in early August and runs through October. Because of their ability to withstand and even thrive in cold storage, however, pears come to market in prime condition right through spring.

The longevity of harvested pears results from a rather odd characteristic: pears do not mature properly if allowed to ripen on the tree. A ripe pear plucked from a branch, in fact, is likely to be gritty. Picked green, stored cold for a month and allowed to ripen on the kitchen counter, however, a pear becomes buttery, juicy and oh, so sweet, with a delicate, elusive flavor.

Ripening pears requires patience on the part of the prospective pear eater. As with bananas and tomatoes, the ripening agent for pears is ethylene gas produced by the pears themselves. Ethylene transforms the starch in pears to sugar, a process that proceeds best at room temperature. Hastening the process can be accomplished by placing pears in a container to trap the gas. A paper bag is ideal.

Most pear varieties don't change color as they ripen. The proper test, then, is touch. When the stem end yields to pressure, a pear is ripe. On the other hand, softness at the blossom end usually means a pear is rotten at the core. Low temperatures retard the ripening process. Storing in the refrigerator is the best way to prevent ripening or to keep ripe pears for a few days before eating.

Pears are roughly, and somewhat inexactly, classified as Bartletts and "winter pears." Bartlett is a variety. Winter pears comprise a number of varieties. The distinction between them used to be clear: The Bartlett was an early pear that didn't store very well and thus was not available in the winter. Winter pears were those varieties that came to market from late autumn through the dead of winter. Both pears and storage conditions have been improved, however, and the distinction is not nearly as useful as it once was.

In Washington, the two most important commercially grown pears are Bartletts and the winter variety known as

PEAR AND WHITE CHOCOLATE MOUSSE

An unusual but irresistible combination, this is a spectacular dessert when served in balloon glasses and topped with dark chocolate shavings.

> 2 pears, peeled, cored and sliced thinly
> 6 tablespoons unsalted butter
> 8 ounces white chocolate, broken in bits
> 4 eggs, separated
> ½ cup superfine sugar
> ⅓ cup amaretto
> 1 envelope unflavored gelatin
> 2 tablespoons cold water
> 1½ cups cream
> 2 tablespoons superfine sugar
> Dark chocolate shavings

1. Make pears into sauce by cooking with 2 tablespoons of the butter over medium heat, stirring frequently, until they are broken up and no liquid remains. Mash. Cool.
2. Melt remaining butter and let cool slightly. In bowl over hot, but not boiling, water, combine melted butter and white chocolate bits and stir until chocolate melts. Do not allow any water to get into mixture. Remove bowl from over hot water and beat butter-chocolate mixture to blend.
3. Beat the egg yolks with the ½ cup superfine sugar in a bowl until the sugar is entirely dissolved and the mixture becomes light-colored and fluffy. Stir in amaretto. Transfer mixture to the top of a double boiler.
4. Bring water in bottom of double boiler to simmer, making certain the top part does not touch the water. Whisk mixture constantly in top of double boiler until mixture holds its shape in a spoon, about 5 minutes. Do not allow mixture to boil. Remove from heat and whisk 2-3 minutes to cool.
5. Process pear sauce, chocolate mixture and egg mixture together 1 minute. Turn mixture into large bowl to cool.
6. Soften gelatin in the 2 tablespoons cold water. Dissolve by placing container holding gelatin in pan of simmering water. Simmer, stirring, until gelatin dissolves. Whisk gelatin in slow stream into the pear-chocolate-egg mixture.
7. Whip cream with the 2 tablespoons of superfine sugar until stiff. Clean beaters and whip egg whites until stiff but not dry.
8. Stir one-quarter of the egg whites into the chocolate mixture. Fold in whipped cream. Fold in remaining egg whites. Pour into serving bowl or individual serving glasses. Refrigerate until set. Serve chilled with dark chocolate shavings as garnish.

Serves 4-6

PEARS WITH MASCARPONE

This dish transforms the fruit-and-cheese course into a dessert.

> 4 ripe pears, peeled, cored and quartered
> 3 tablespoons pear brandy
> ½ cup mascarpone
> ½ cup sour cream
> Honey
> ½ cup cream

1. Slice pear quarters thinly crosswise. Toss slices immediately with pear brandy. Refrigerate 1 hour or more.
2. Process or blend mascarpone and sour cream, sweetened with honey to taste, until smooth.
3. Whip cream lightly and sweeten with honey to taste.
4. To serve, combine pears with cheese mixture and spoon cream over.

Serves 4-6

Darleen Wheeler of Walla Walla paring pears.

Anjou. Bartletts are the country's best-known and most popular pear, and they're also the pear most often found in cans. They comprise about a third of Washington's crop, and 70 percent of them are canned. The Bartlett harvest begins about the second week of August and lasts a month. Those Bartletts that go to the fresh market are usually sold before the end of November, although some are stored under special conditions and are available for another month or so.

A Bartlett is a beautiful pear, one of the rare ones that turns color as it ripens. Green in the unripened state, a Bartlett ripens into a rich yellow, sometimes with a red blush. One type of Bartlett, in fact, is called Red Bartlett and has been enjoying increased popularity as researchers improve the brilliance of the color. Though some fanciers will argue, the consensus seems to be that Red Bartletts don't taste any different than their yellow cousins. They do currently cost more, though, as red pear types wax popular and demand outstrips supply.

All pears are excellent for eating out of hand. Some are better for cooking than others, however. Bartletts fit into the second category since they hold their shape well when baked or poached.

Though precise statistics are hard to come by, Washington's leading pear is the Anjou, accounting for nearly half the state's crop. Anjous are somewhat egg-shaped, green in color and mild in flavor.

As with all winter pears, their harvest begins in mid-September and lasts through October. Some Anjous come to market more or less directly from the orchard, but, like other winter varieties, they seem to improve with a month or so of cold storage. Anjous don't change color as they ripen. And they are not an especially good cooking pear, though they work well in salads.

The other principal winter-pear variety grown in Washington is the Bosc. Pear sales generally are increasing in this country, but perhaps no pear is growing in popularity as rapidly as the Bosc. As consumers have become more discriminating in pear selection, the Bosc has overcome its one consumer drawback: russeting, in which the skin becomes brown and rough. Unlike Europeans, Americans seem put off by russeted fruit, an unfortunate tendency that means not only that they miss much that the fruit world has to offer, but also that growers concentrate on prettier but often lesser fruit varieties.

Pear fanciers know, however, that the Bosc is an exceptional pear. Certainly its looks are distinctive: a long neck and a gracefully curving stem. The Bosc is also among the sweetest of pears, second only to the Comice. Gritty in the unripened state, a Bosc's flesh becomes creamy as it ripens. Even ripe, though, its texture is firmer than most varieties', and the Bosc, consequently, is the ideal pear for cooking when shape retention is important. Though a Bosc's russet skin is not harmful

FRENCH PEAR PIE

Guests at Moreland's restaurant in Spokane badger owner Billie Moreland for her recipes, but she doesn't give them out. The recipe for this sumptuous dessert is among those most in demand. Here, for the first time, it's disclosed publicly.

Poached Pears

4 cups white wine
2 cups sugar
Juice of half a lemon
4 pears, peeled, halved and cored

Pastry

2¼ cups flour
1 teaspoon salt
¼ cup plus 1 tablespoon milk
9 tablespoons vegetable oil

Filling

3 tablespoons flour
½ cup sugar
¼ teaspoon ground ginger
1½ cups sour cream

Topping

½ cup flour
¼ cup sugar
½ teaspoon nutmeg
¼ cup chilled butter

1. Poach pears by combining wine, sugar and lemon juice in a noncorrosive pan and boiling for 10 minutes. Add pear halves and simmer for 10-30 minutes (depending on ripeness), until they pierce easily with knife. Remove pears and cool, reserving liquid for reuse.
2. Prepare pastry by sifting flour and salt into a bowl. Combine milk and vegetable oil but don't stir. Pour mixture all at once into flour. Mix and form into a ball. Divide in half. (This recipe makes two crusts. Freeze unused half or make 2 pies.) Roll half the dough between sheets of waxed paper into ⅛-inch-thick circle. Press dough into 9-inch pie pan.
3. Prepare filling by mixing flour, sugar and ginger. Add sour cream and mix thoroughly.
4. Prepare topping by mixing dry ingredients and cutting in butter until mixture is mealy.
5. Arrange pear halves on pastry. Pour in sour cream mixture. Sprinkle on topping. Bake at 400°F for 25-30 minutes, until pie is golden brown.

Serves 6

SPICED PEAR BREAD

Coarse-ground whole-wheat flour gives this sweet bread a grainier, better texture.

1 cup whole-wheat flour
1½ cups white flour
1 teaspoon baking powder
1 teaspoon baking soda
1 teaspoon salt
2 teaspoons cinnamon
¼ teaspoon grated nutmeg
¼ teaspoon ground ginger
1 large pear, peeled, cored and chopped
½ cup chopped pecans
3 tablespoons margarine
    (or shortening), softened
½ cup packed brown sugar
2 eggs, beaten lightly
1 cup buttermilk

1. Mix dry ingredients together well. Stir in chopped pear and nuts.
2. Cream margarine (or shortening) with brown sugar. Beat in eggs. Beat in buttermilk.
3. Add dry ingredients to wet ingredients and stir just to combine.
4. Scrape batter into large buttered loaf pan. Bake at 375°F for 45-50 minutes, until wood pick inserted in middle comes out dry.
5. Cool bread in pan on rack 10-12 minutes, loosen edges with knife, invert on rack and remove. Let cool 30 minutes before slicing.

or unpleasant in taste, it is, unlike the Anjou's, somewhat tough, and many Bosc fanciers prefer to peel it.

Several other winter-pear varieties are grown in Washington, but in relatively small numbers. Among them are the little Seckels, whose size makes them popular for preserving whole in, say, brandy or a spicy syrup; small, bell-shaped Forelles; and the superb Comices.

Preferences among pear varieties are as numerous as the varieties themselves. Unarguably, however, the Comice is the sweetest pear there is. Rounded and chubby in shape, a Comice changes color slightly as it ripens, becoming less green and more yellow, sometimes with a crimson blush. Certain types achieve great size and are highly prized. Ripening a Comice properly and carefully is well worth the time, since the flesh becomes as smooth as butter and supremely juicy. (Unfortunately, the latter quality rules the Comice out as a prime cooking pear.) Aficionados insist that a well-ripened Comice should not be peeled but cut in half and scooped out with a spoon.

The Comice is a tricky pear to grow and requires certain climatic conditions. Consequently, few are grown commercially in Washington, and most Comice sold in Washington markets come from the Medford and Hood River areas of Oregon.

The Comice aside, Washington offers a wide range of pear choices, and cultivating a discriminating taste for them amply rewards the effort.

PEAR TART

This is a rich tart with farmhouse flavor.

1⅓ cup sugar
6 tablespoons flour
3 eggs, beaten lightly
12 tablespoons butter
2 pears, peeled, cored and quartered
1 9-inch tart shell (see below)
Powdered sugar

1. Beat sugar, flour and eggs until smooth. Melt butter over medium-high heat in skillet and cook until lightly browned. Gradually whisk melted butter into sugar-egg mixture.
2. Cut each pear quarter into several thin slices, then fan open slices to resemble flower petals. Arrange petal shapes in tart shell.
3. Pour batter over pears. Bake at 375°F for about 1 hour. Serve warm or at room temperature, sprinkling with powdered sugar.

Serves 6-8

Tart Shell

1½ cups flour
1½ tablespoons sugar
Pinch salt
2 teaspoons lemon juice
1 egg yolk
10 tablespoons unsalted butter, chilled and cut into bits
2-3 tablespoons ice water

1. Combine flour, sugar and salt in processor and process until mixed. Add lemon juice and egg yolk and process to blend. Add butter and process until mixture breaks into pea-size bits. Add ice water a little at a time until dough masses around blade.
2. Remove dough from processor and form into ball. Cover with plastic wrap and chill until firm, about 30 minutes. (Dough may be frozen and brought to room temperature before rolling out.)
3. Roll out dough to cover 9-inch tart pan with removable rim. Press dough into flutes on rim and trim along top.
4. Prick shell all over with fork. Line shell with waxed paper and fill paper with dried beans or rice. Bake at 350°F for 15 minutes. Remove beans or rice and waxed paper. Bake about 15 minutes more, until shell is pale gold. Cool on rack. Brush with syrup made by dissolving 3 tablespoons sugar in 2 tablespoons water and boiling 5 minutes, brushing crystals from sides of pan as syrup cooks.
5. Return shell to oven 5 minutes to set.

PEARS IN RED WINE

Many varieties of pear poach into a dessert of rare beauty with this method. Make certain the pears are all equally ripe so their cooking time is the same. And watch them carefully; cooking time varies greatly according to the pears' ripeness.

4 pears, peeled, cored and quartered
2 cups red wine
½ cup sugar
2 tablespoons lemon juice
Peel of 1 lemon
1-2 tablespoons brandy (optional)

1. Place all ingredients except the brandy in a pan and bring to boil. Cover and simmer for 10-30 minutes (depending on ripeness), until pears pierce easily with knife.
2. Remove pears and reduce cooking liquid to about ⅔ cup. Add brandy after reducing, if desired. Recombine pears and syrup and cool. Serve at room temperature or chilled.

Serves 4-6

BAKED PEARS

This version of baked pears is slightly more elaborate than the following version.

½ cup seedless raisins
⅓ cup brown sugar
1 teaspoon lemon zest
1 tablespoon brandy
4 pears, peeled, halved and cored
1 cup sweet white wine
Additional brandy for flaming

1. Mix raisins, brown sugar, lemon zest and brandy.
2. Arrange pears cut side up in buttered casserole. Spoon mixture into cavities and pour white wine around.
3. Cover casserole and bake at 350°F for 30-40 minutes, until pears are tender.
4. Warm ¼ to ½ cup brandy in small pan, ignite and pour over pears. Serve warm.

Serves 4-8

CARIBBEAN BAKED PEARS

Rum and lime lend the flavor of the West Indies to this dessert.

1 teaspoon lime juice
1 teaspoon honey
1 tablespoon rum
2 tablespoons chopped walnuts
4 pears, peeled, halved and cored

Basting Sauce

2 tablespoons lime juice
2 tablespoons honey
2 tablespoons rum
2 tablespoons water

1. Mix lime juice, honey, rum and walnuts.
2. Arrange pears in a buttered casserole with cut side up. Spoon the mixture into cavities.

3. Cover casserole and bake at 350°F for 25-30 minutes, until pears are nearly tender. Prepare basting sauce by mixing all ingredients, and baste pears two or three times during baking.
4. Uncover pears and brown them lightly under broiler. Serve warm.

Serves 4-8

PEAR SALAD WITH GORGONZOLA

Here's a pear salad that features Gorgonzola, the Italian blue cheese.

1 bunch watercress
1 head Bibb lettuce
2 pears, peeled, cored and sliced
¼ pound Gorgonzola
¼ cup pine nuts
Creamy vinaigrette (see below)

1. Rinse, drain and dry watercress and lettuce. Tear into bite-size pieces. Mix and arrange on plates.
2. Arrange pear slices over greens, crumble Gorgonzola over pears and sprinkle on pine nuts. Serve with creamy vinaigrette.

Serves 4-6

Creamy Vinaigrette

2 egg yolks
2 teaspoons Dijon-style mustard
1 clove garlic, minced
½ teaspoon minced fresh coriander
¼ cup red wine vinegar
Salt and pepper
1 cup olive oil

Whip egg yolks until frothy. Beat in all other ingredients except oil. Whip in oil little by little.

POACHED PEARS WITH RASPBERRY SAUCE

In this recipe, the pears are poached in white wine and the raspberry sauce provides the color. It's a beautiful dessert, suitable for a special dinner party. Bosc pears are perfect for the dish, but Bartletts do nicely, too. The star anise, offered as an option in the recipe, is available at Asian specialty shops.

> 6 cups white wine
> 3 cups sugar
>   Juice of lemon
> 1 stick cinnamon
> 2 star anise (optional)
> 6 pears
>   Raspberry sauce (see below)

1. In a noncorrosive pan, combine wine, sugar, lemon juice, cinnamon stick and star anise. Boil 10 minutes.
2. Peel the pears and either leave whole or halve and core with a melon-ball cutter. Poach pears at simmer in wine mixture 10-30 minutes (depending on ripeness), until they almost pierce easily with knife (they'll continue cooking in liquid). Remove from heat and cool in liquid. Chill and serve.
3. To serve, puddle a little raspberry sauce on a dish, place pear in the puddle and spoon more sauce on top.

Serves 6-12

Raspberry Sauce

> 4 cups frozen raspberries, thawed
>   Sugar
> 2 tablespoons kirsch (or 1 tablespoon lemon juice)

Drain raspberries and process with sugar to taste until smooth. Strain through fine sieve. Add kirsch (or lemon juice) and chill.

POACHED PEARS WITH CHOCOLATE SAUCE

This poaching liquid, unlike the others (there are 3) in this chapter, is a simple syrup. Here the pears are crowned with chocolate, for which they have an affinity.

> 4 pears, peeled, stems left on
>   Lemon juice
> ¼ cup sugar
> 2 cups water

Chocolate Sauce

> 4 squares semi-sweet chocolate
> 2 tablespoons butter

1. Brush peeled pears immediately with lemon juice so they don't discolor. Dissolve sugar in water over medium-low heat. Poach pears in syrup, covered, at simmer 10-30 minutes (depending on ripeness), until they pierce easily with knife.
2. Remove pears from syrup. Chill.
3. Reduce syrup by boiling to about ¼ cup. Melt chocolate in hot syrup, stirring. Remove from heat and beat until smooth. Beat butter into hot syrup.
4. To serve, arrange chilled pears upright on serving platter, warm chocolate sauce and pour over pears.

Serves 4

Poached
Pears with
Raspberry
Sauce

Poached
Pears with
Chocolate
Sauce

PEAR, SMOKED CHICKEN AND WALNUT SALAD

Pears make a superb salad ingredient, as this enticing combination demonstrates.

4 pears, peeled, cored and quartered
½ cup sugar
⅓ cup coarsely chopped walnuts
4 halves smoked chicken breasts
Assorted salad greens
Walnut vinaigrette (see below)

1. Poach pears in syrup of the sugar and water to cover. Simmer 10-30 minutes (depending on ripeness), until pears pierce easily with knife. Remove from liquid and cool.
2. Toast walnuts in 325°F oven about 20 minutes, shaking pan occasionally.
3. Skin chicken breasts. Slice thinly on a slant across grain. Cut pear quarters in half lengthwise. Alternate pears and chicken slices attractively on half the plate. Arrange torn salad greens, such as Belgian endive, watercress, arugula and Bibb lettuce, on the other half. Drizzle walnut vinaigrette over all and sprinkle with walnuts.

Serves 6

Walnut Vinaigrette

1 tablespoon Dijon-style mustard
1 egg yolk
⅓ cup red wine vinegar
Salt and pepper
1 cup walnut oil

Whisk mustard into egg yolk. Mix in vinegar, salt and pepper to taste. Gradually whisk in walnut oil.

PEARS, BEANS AND BACON POT

Side dish or main course, this hearty fare fortifies against winter weather.

1 pound dried white beans,
soaked overnight
1 pound slab bacon in 1-inch dice
½ cup finely chopped onions
¼ cup finely chopped celery
4 pears, peeled, cored and chunked
Salt and pepper

1. Simmer beans in 3 cups water, covered, for 30 minutes.
2. Meanwhile, brown bacon dice on all sides over low heat. Remove and reserve. Sauté onions and celery in bacon fat for 10-12 minutes, until quite tender.
3. Add bacon, vegetables, fat and pears to beans. Salt and pepper to taste. Simmer covered about 90 minutes, until beans are tender. Mash pears by stirring through beans thoroughly. Serve hot.

Serves 4-6

PEAR-RUTABAGA PUREE

A slightly sweet side dish, this puree goes nicely with poultry or pork.

2 pears, peeled, cored and quartered
1 tablespoon lemon juice
1 pound rutabagas, peeled and chunked
4 tablespoons butter
¼ cup cream
Salt and pepper

1. Simmer pears with lemon juice in water to cover for 10-30 minutes (depending on ripeness), until they pierce easily with knife. Drain.
2. Meanwhile, sauté rutabagas in butter over low heat for 20-25 minutes, until tender.
3. Process pears and rutabagas with cooking butter, adding cream as necessary to make smooth puree. Salt and pepper to taste. Return to stove and just heat through.

Serves 1

# POTATOES

POTATOES

It's something of a secret, but the plain truth is that Washington produces the best baking potatoes in the world. And a lot of them, too. Yes, Idaho has excellent potatoes, and it's still the country's largest producer of what are known as "fall potatoes"—that is, the big baking variety. In terms of both acreage and production, Washington ranks second to Idaho. Nevertheless, a case can be made that Washington is a better potato state than Idaho. If it were not for apples, in fact, Washington's reputation might well rest on the homely spud.

Washington's potato business didn't really begin on a large scale until the mid-1950s, when substantial tracts of irrigated land became available in the Columbia Basin. From 25,000 acres in those days, the potato business has grown to 100,000-plus acres. That's only one-third of Idaho's potato acreage. But Washington's yield per acre is the highest in the world, more than twice Idaho's. And Washington's baking potatoes are a bit less watery and therefore are somewhat better than Idaho's.

The reason for this is Central Washington's ideal potato-growing climate: long sunny days and cool evenings (and a longer frost-free growing season than Idaho's). The sunny days promote the development of starch in the potato plant's leaves. The cool evenings trigger the "translocation" of the starch to the plant's roots, or tubers. Washington potato farms average some 500 100-pound sacks of potatoes per acre. That's about five billion pounds of potatoes annually, nearly 20 percent of the nation's fall-potato production. "Potato Country USA" is what Washington potato growers call their rich lands, in an effort to gain some well-deserved recognition.

Washington's reputation as a potato state rests on its production of russet varieties, those "baking potato" types with russeted skins and solid, mealy flesh. About 97 percent of Washington's commercial crop is russets, and the preeminent one is the Russet Burbank.

First on the market each year, however, is the Norgold Russet. Norgolds, a "short-season," early potato, are harvested from early July to early September. They constitute about 12 percent of Washington's commercial crop. Most are sold fresh, as opposed to processed.

Russet Burbanks make up about 85 percent of the commercial crop. Their harvest begins about the time that the Norgolds' ends and lasts until mid-October. Russet Burbanks for the fresh market go immediately into storage and emerge when the market has consumed the Norgolds. Then they are sold fresh throughout

STUFFED POTATOES

Stuffing, or twice-baking, is a good way of embellishing prime russet potatoes. Stuffing combinations are unlimited. Here are two suggestions rich enough to be served as a main course as well as a side dish.

Ham and Egg Stuffing

    4 large russet potatoes
      Vegetable oil
    2 whole eggs
    2 egg yolks
    6 tablespoons butter
    ½ cup cream
      Salt and pepper
    ½ cup minced onion
    1 cup minced cooked ham
    2 tablespoons minced chives or
      green pepper
    1 cup shredded Jarlsberg cheese

1. Scrub potatoes, dry and rub lightly with vegetable oil. Prick several times with fork. Bake at 425°F for about 1 hour, until tender when pressed.
2. Cut a slice lengthwise from each potato. Scoop out the pulp and reserve shells.
3. Combine potato pulp with eggs and yolks. Mix in 4 tablespoons of the butter, cream, salt and pepper to taste. Whip until smooth.
4. Sauté onion over low heat in remaining butter 5-6 minutes. Add ham and chives or green pepper. Sauté gently 5 minutes. Stir into potato mixture. Fold in most of cheese, reserving some for topping.
5. Pack stuffing into potato shells, using a pastry bag with a star tube if you desire. Top with reserved cheese.
6. Reheat in 450°F oven 10-15 minutes, and then brown under broiler. Serve immediately.

Serves 4-8

Mushroom and Bacon Stuffing

    4 large russet potatoes
      Vegetable oil
    ½ pound sliced bacon, sliced crosswise
      in 1-inch pieces
    4 tablespoons butter
    ½ cup finely chopped onion
    2 cups chopped button mushrooms
    ½ cup sour cream
    ½ cup grated cheddar cheese
      Salt and pepper

1. Scrub potatoes, dry and rub lightly with vegetable oil. Prick several times with fork. Bake at 425°F for about 1 hour, until tender when pressed.
2. Cut a slice lengthwise from each of the potatoes. Scoop out the pulp and reserve shells.
3. Meanwhile, sauté bacon until crisp. Remove and drain. Remove all but 2 tablespoons of the fat from skillet. Add butter and sauté onion 8-10 minutes, until limp but not brown. Add mushrooms and sauté until their liquid has evaporated.
4. Combine potato pulp and onion-mushroom mixture. Stir in sour cream and most of cheese, reserving some for topping. Salt and pepper to taste.
5. Pack stuffing into potato shells, using a pastry bag with a star tube if you desire. Top with reserved cheese.
6. Reheat in 450°F oven 10-15 minutes, and then brown under broiler. Serve immediately.

Serves 4-8

Larry Hector of Prescott offering potatoes.

the winter and up until about June 1. The bulk of Russet Burbanks, however, are processed into frozen French fries and dehydrated products, principally in the nine major potato-processing plants that Washington growers support in their own state.

It takes an expert to tell the difference between Norgolds and Russet Burbanks. Norgolds tend to be less oval in shape, but that's often hard to discern. The best method of distinguishing russets is by season. In the late summer and early fall, potatoes sold as "Washington Russets" will be Norgolds. By December or, at the latest,

January 1, they will be Russet Burbanks. For home cooks, the difference between the two is marginal. Norgolds have two to three percent more water and are less solid, making the Russet Burbank slightly superior for baking and French frying.

When buying potatoes, avoid those that have begun to "green" from exposure to light. Greening produces bitterness and toxicity. If potatoes do have green areas, cut them off. Unless you have proper facilities, storing large numbers of potatoes for long periods of time is not a good idea. Let the experts store them and buy as your

POTATOES O'BRIEN

The origin of this dish is unknown to George O'Leary, administrator of the Washington State Potato Commission, but he well remembers, while growing up in Idaho, helping his mother prepare it in massive amounts for dozens of community dinners. Potatoes O'Brien's fame has not diminished since its transplantation to Washington, only now the recipe's curator is O'Leary's wife, Joan. This recipe feeds a farm family plus the hired hands. Halve it for a normal-size family.

6 large russet potatoes, peeled
1 pound bacon or ham or a combination
1 large onion
1 small jar pimientos
½ pound sharp cheddar cheese
 Salt and pepper
 Milk

1. Grind potatoes, bacon, onion, pimientos and cheese together coarsely. Salt and pepper to taste. Pack into greased baking dish. Pour in enough milk to cover.
2. Bake at 350°F for 90 minutes.

Serves 8-10

POTATO-LEEK PIE

Marriage to the elegant leek lends the humble potato a certain nobility. Serve this as an accompaniment to any meat or poultry dish.

3 large russet potatoes, peeled
2 large leeks
1 large onion
1 teaspoon dried thyme
1 teaspoon salt
½ cup chopped parsley
 White pepper
½ cup dried whole-wheat bread crumbs
4 tablespoons melted butter

1. Cut potatoes into chunks. Trim leeks of dark green parts, split in half, clean thoroughly and cut into chunks. Peel onion and cut into chunks.
2. Place potatoes, leeks, onion, thyme and salt in pan. Pour in water to nearly cover, about 5 cups. Simmer, covered, for 30 minutes.
3. Uncover, increase heat and boil about 15 minutes, stirring to prevent burning, until most of the liquid has evaporated.
4. Remove from heat. Stir in parsley and white pepper. Adjust salt to taste.
5. Spoon mixture into buttered baking dish. Sprinkle on bread crumbs. Dribble melted butter over all. Bake at 350°F for 15-20 minutes, until top is golden. Serve hot.

Serves 6-8

POTATO AND KALE SOUP

Here's an adaptation of a classic Portuguese soup. Try it with a sprinkle of the topping suggested below.

4 russet potatoes, peeled and diced
6 cups beef or chicken stock
 Salt and pepper
½ pound cured sausage
½ pound kale, stems removed and finely shredded

1. Combine potatoes, stock and salt and pepper to taste. Bring to boil and simmer briskly about 15 minutes, until potatoes are quite tender. Remove two-thirds of the potatoes, mash and return to pot.
2. Slice sausage of choice into 1/4-inch rounds. Add to pot and heat through several minutes. Add kale and simmer 3-4 minutes.

Serves 4-6

Note: For a savory addition, combine 2 tablespoons minced parsley, 1 teaspoon minced garlic and 2 tablespoons bread crumbs. Moisten with olive oil. Sprinkle on soup servings.

Potatoes
O'Brien

Potato-Leek
Pie

Potato and
Kale Soup

needs dictate. If you do want to store baking-type potatoes, the ideal conditions are in a dark place at 45°F and high humidity.

Because they are so high in solids, Washington's Russet Burbanks are unsurpassed for baking and French frying. (While not as good as their cousins, Norgolds are, nonetheless, the best baking type available in Washington during their season, far superior to those trucked in from, say, California.)

Properly baking a potato is simple. Just scrub the skin, rub it with oil if you like a soft skin, pierce it several times with a fork (to make steam vents) and pop it into a 400°F oven for 50 to 60 minutes. Test for doneness by squeezing. Slit lengthwise and push the ends toward the center to expose the flesh. Do not bake potatoes by wrapping them in foil. You'll steam them that way, and you want a dry, fluffy baked potato, not something akin to being boiled and mashed.

French frying is more complicated. Since the Washington Russet Burbank absorbs little oil and produces rigid, crisp French fries rather than the all-too-common limp, soggy ones, however, it's worth the effort. Choose a good oil that won't burn at high temperatures. Peanut is best, but expensive. Soybean or even cottonseed is fine. Scrub the potatoes and peel them if you wish. Slice them to the thickness you prefer. Then soak the slices in ice water for 20 to 30 minutes to rid them of surface starch, which will cause uneven browning and cloud the oil. Dry the slices thoroughly. Heat the oil to 375°F. Fry the potato slices a few at a time for about seven minutes, until they are brown. Drain and salt. Do not salt them over the frying oil since salt breaks down the oil. (Properly handled, the oil can be used more than once, especially if no water or salt gets in it. Simply strain the oil through cheesecloth and store it in the refrigerator.)

An even better method of French frying is to cook the potatoes twice. The first time should be at 360°F for about five minutes. Do not brown at this stage. Drain the slices and allow them to cool to room temperature. (They may be held for a couple of hours awaiting the second cooking or even stored in the refrigerator, covered, overnight. Or they may be wrapped and frozen. Just remember to bring them to room temperature before the second frying.) The second dunking in the hot oil is actually just for browning. Bring the oil to 390°F this time and fry the slices for about two minutes. Drain and salt.

Russet potatoes are not ideal for all uses. They break up in potato salads, for instance, and don't pan-fry well. Waxy "boiling potatoes," of course, are the better choice for cold salads or for any other cooking use in which it's important that the cut-up potatoes retain their shape.

In the accompanying recipes, baking potatoes are preferred.

One final note: Eating raw potatoes won't hurt you, but won't help you, either. For the starch of a potato to become digestible, it must be cooked.

POTATO GRATIN

The French consider this dish a cultural virtue. The potatoes must be sliced as thin as dimes.

1 cup grated Gruyère cheese
1 cup milk
1 cup crème fraiche (see Notes on
* Ingredients, page xi)*
* Salt and pepper*
2 pounds russet potatoes, peeled

1. Combine ¾ cup of the Gruyère with the milk and crème fraiche. Salt and pepper to taste. Slice potatoes thinly into mixture and stir to coat slices.
2. Spoon potatoes into buttered baking dish with slotted spoon, leveling them as much as possible. Pour the milk-cream mixture over potatoes. Sprinkle on the remaining Gruyère.
3. Bake at 375°F for 70-80 minutes, until top is browned.

Serves 4-6

POTATO CRISPS

Making these glorified potato chips requires a supply of clarified butter and careful attention so the potatoes don't burn.

1½ pounds russet potatoes, peeled
12 tablespoons clarified butter
* Salt*

1. Trim potatoes into smooth cylinders. Slice crosswise very thinly and drop slices into ice water. Soak for at least 30 minutes, changing the water at least once.
2. Drain potato slices and pat dry. Spread evenly in large roasting pan. Pour clarified butter over potatoes.
3. Bake at 450°F for 20 minutes. Remove pan from oven and pour off butter. Return to oven and bake 5 minutes more, without burning. Salt to taste and serve immediately.

Serves 4

ROESTI POTATOES

This is a variation of a classic Swiss dish. Here, it's made thinner, and bits of sweet red pepper and scallion are added for color and flavor.

3 large russet potatoes (4 cups
* after shredding)*
6 tablespoons butter, melted
½ cup finely chopped scallion
½ cup finely chopped sweet red pepper
* Salt and pepper*
¼ cup minced parsley

1. Boil unpeeled potatoes about 3 minutes, drain and peel. Shred.
2. In a heavy 8-inch skillet, place 2 tablespoons of the butter, then make thin layer of shredded potatoes. Sprinkle potatoes with some of the scallion and red pepper. Salt and pepper lightly. Dribble on some of the butter. Continue layering until all the potatoes are used.
3. Cover potatoes with foil and a lid slightly smaller than skillet. Place on medium heat and, when butter sizzles, press down firmly to make potato cake. Cook 5 minutes. Shake pan over heat and cook 20 minutes, until bottom of potato cake is browned.
4. Flip potato cake onto dish and slide unbrowned side into bottom of skillet. Turn up heat to medium-high and fry 5-6 minutes, until underside is browned, too. Sprinkle with parsley, cut into wedges and serve.

Serves 4-6

Potato
Gratin

Potato
Crisps

Roesti
Potatoes

GNOCCHI WITH PESTO

Two wonders of Italian cuisine come together in this dish, which Italians would eat as a first course but Americans might prefer as a main course. The accompanying pesto recipe is one of many for this classic Genovese sauce.

> 1¾ cups white flour
> 1 pound russet potatoes, boiled
>   and peeled
> Salt
> Pesto (see below)
> Grated Parmesan

1. Spread flour on board. Pass potatoes through ricer directly onto the flour. Sprinkle with a pinch of salt. Knead flour into potatoes until dough is firm. Knead about 5 minutes more.
2. Cut dough into several pieces and roll each piece into long, thin roll about ½ inch in diameter. Slice each roll into 1-inch pieces.
3. Shape the gnocchi this way: Grasp fork in one hand, with tines pressed against flat surface. With the other hand, place a piece of dough on the fork's face. Press on the top of the dough with your thumb just firmly enough to leave an impression. Roll the dough gently across the tines onto the flat surface. The tines will leave a light impression on the underside of the dumpling and the thumb impression will make the top slightly concave.
4. Drop gnocchi into a large pot of boiling, salted water. When they rise to the top, remove with slotted spoon and place in shallow, warm, buttered dish. Immediately spoon on generous amount of room-temperature pesto and serve with grated Parmesan.

Serves 4-6

Pesto

> 3 cups fresh basil leaves, stems removed
> 3 cloves garlic, chopped
> 2 tablespoons pine nuts
> 1 teaspoon salt
>   Pepper
> 1 cup olive oil
> ½ cup grated Parmesan
> ½ cup grated Romano (or double
>   Parmesan)
> 4 tablespoons butter, softened

1. Briefly chop basil, garlic, pine nuts, salt and pepper in processor. Scrape down sides of bowl. Turn on processor and add oil quickly in a steady stream through feeder tube. Do not cream—basil should end up being minced.
2. Transfer to bowl and mix in cheeses and butter. If sauce seems too thick, add ¼ cup more oil and mix well.

Note: *Pesto can be stored in the refrigerator in a covered jar indefinitely. Just top the sauce with olive oil after each use. Pesto can also be frozen.*

POTATOES AND SAUERKRAUT

This dish, as rustic as it sounds, provides robust flavor in minutes.

> 2 cups sauerkraut
> 8 slices bacon, chopped coarsely
> ½ cup minced onion
> 2 cups mashed potatoes
> ½ cup chicken stock
>   Salt and pepper

1. Rinse sauerkraut as necessary to reduce sourness to taste. Squeeze out excess water and fluff up.
2. Fry bacon bits over medium heat for several minutes, add onions and fry 2 minutes more, until tender. Add sauerkraut and cook 5 minutes.
3. Add potatoes, mix well, cover and cook 5 minutes. Add chicken stock, salt and pepper to taste, re-cover and cook 5 minutes.

Serves 4-6

MASHED POTATOES LOADED WITH GARLIC

Don't recoil, the garlic won't blow your head off in this dish. It's mellowed long before it's combined with potatoes.

    2 heads garlic
    5 tablespoons butter
    2 tablespoons flour
    1 cup milk, boiling
      Salt and pepper
2½ pounds russet potatoes
    4 tablespoons butter, softened
    4 tablespoons cream
    4 tablespoons minced parsley

1. Break up garlic heads and peel cloves whole. Cook whole cloves with the 5 tablespoons butter in skillet over low heat until very tender but not browned, about 20 minutes. Stir frequently.
2. Sprinkle flour over garlic and stir 1-2 minutes, but do not brown. Remove from heat and stir in boiling milk. Salt and pepper lightly. Return to heat and boil 1 minute. Puree in blender, processor or food mill. Return to heat and cook 2 minutes.
3. Peel and cut up potatoes. Boil in lightly salted water until tender. Then drain and mash.
4. Return to heat and cook 2 minutes, stirring vigorously to evaporate moisture. Remove from heat and beat in the 4 tablespoons softened butter.
5. Beat hot garlic mixture into mashed potatoes. Beat in cream. Stir in parsley. Salt and pepper to taste.

Serves 6-8

CREAMED POTATOES WITH TWO CHEESES

Here is a savory accompaniment to all sorts of roasted meats.

    2 pounds russet potatoes, peeled
      and diced
    5 tablespoons butter
    5 tablespoons flour
    2 cups cream, scalded
⅔ cup chicken stock
      Salt and pepper
    5 tablespoons grated Parmesan
½ cup Roquefort cheese, crumbled
½ cup melted butter
      Paprika

1. Parboil potato dice 5 minutes. Drain.
2. Melt 5 tablespoons butter in small pan over low heat. When it stops foaming, beat in flour and cook, stirring, 2 minutes without allowing to color. Remove from heat and pour in scalded cream all at once, beating to blend. Add chicken stock and return to medium-high heat. Stirring, bring to boil, reduce heat and simmer, stirring, 10 minutes, until thickened. Remove from heat, salt and pepper to taste and stir in Parmesan to dissolve.
3. Fold potatoes into sauce. Divide mixture among 6 buttered ramekins. Sprinkle each with Roquefort, melted butter and paprika.
4. Bake at 425°F for 15 minutes.

Serves 6

Potato
Pudding
with Dried
Fruit

Mediter-
ranean
Potatoes

POTATO PUDDING WITH DRIED FRUIT

Slightly sweet, this side dish is a good accompaniment to poultry, pork or ham.

　2 eggs
　2 egg yolks
　3 large russet potatoes, boiled and
　　　mashed
　½ cup cornmeal
　½ cup butter, softened
　　Salt and pepper
　½ pound bacon, diced
　1 cup finely chopped dried fruit, such as
　　　apples, apricots, pears and peaches

1. Lightly beat eggs and egg yolks. Thoroughly mix eggs, mashed potatoes, cornmeal, butter and salt and pepper to taste.
2. Sauté bacon over low heat until barely crisp. Drain and stir into potato mixture. Pour off most of fat from skillet, add fruit and cook 1-2 minutes.
3. Spoon half the potato mixture into deep, buttered baking dish. Level top. Spread on fruit evenly. Pack remainder of potato mixture on top.
4. Place baking dish in large pan. Pour in boiling water to reach halfway up sides of dish. Bake at 325°F for 90 minutes, until skewer thrust in pudding comes out clean.

Serves 4-6

MEDITERRANEAN POTATOES

The taste of Mediterranean cooking comes through in this dish, which, as you'll see below, works as a soup, also.

　　1 bunch chard
　1½ slices stale French bread
　　18 blanched almonds
　3-4 cloves garlic, peeled
　　2 tablespoons coarsely chopped parsley
　　¾ cup olive oil
　1½ cups water
　　7 russet potatoes, peeled and cubed
　1½ cups chicken stock
　　　Salt and pepper

1. Blanch chard in boiling water 1-2 minutes. Immediately plunge into cold water to preserve color. Drain.
2. Sauté bread, almonds, garlic and parsley in the oil over medium-low heat until golden. Remove from skillet with slotted spoon. Add chard to skillet and sauté 1-2 minutes. Drain and reserve oil.
3. Process bread mixture until well combined. Add water and process a few seconds. Add chard and process a few seconds, just to chop.
4. Combine potatoes, chicken stock, reserved oil and bread-chard mixture in pan. Cook over medium heat until potatoes are tender. Salt and pepper to taste. Serve hot.

Serves 6-8

Note: By adding more chicken stock and pureeing when the potatoes are cooked, then reheating, you can make this into an excellent soup.

SALMON

SALMON

To outsiders, nothing marks Washingtonians more distinctively than our relationship with salmon. Most people think of salmon as a rare delicacy, a luxury. For us, at least in others' minds, salmon is a staple, readily available and inexpensive to boot. No wonder they envy us.

There's some truth in that stereotype. Certainly when man first set foot here, he learned what the bears and eagles already knew: the waters, fresh and salt, rinsing our shores were the natural home of what would become the world's most gustatorily prized fish. To the coastal Indians, salmon were life itself, to be treated with awe, reverence and, above all, care.

But the relationship between Washingtonians and salmon is now strained to a degree unknown to most outsiders—even to many Washingtonians. Development, dams, pollution, overfishing, lax management and battles against Indians' fishing rights have depleted Washington's once mighty salmon runs. Our salmon are now threatened with the same fate that befell the bison of the Great Plains.

Still, compared to elsewhere, salmon are indeed readily available in our markets. And their price actually is relatively low. Sadly, the supply and price too often are determined by salmon being caught in Alaskan waters rather than our own.

One consequence of this seems to be that, as cooks, we are more careful of the salmon we buy. Precautions are necessary, we have learned, because salmon reaching the market often are of unreliable quality. A few crusading fishermen have even taught us that frozen salmon can be better than those sold as fresh.

The label "fresh," in fact, is hardly any help at all in buying salmon. It simply means that the fish haven't been frozen. But it also can mean that the fish have been allowed to beat themselves to death on a boat deck, dumped into a hold without being cleaned and steeped in bloody water for days before being brought ashore and taken to market. Unless you catch a salmon yourself, kill, bleed and clean it immediately and chill it properly, you either must locate a fishmonger you can trust or approach a fish market as deliberately as Sherlock Holmes did a crime scene.

The telltale clues are the same for all five species of Pacific salmon: chinook (or king); coho (or silver); sockeye (or red); pink (or humpback); and chum (or dog). The different species vary considerably in flavor, however.

Chinook are the most prized and the largest, sometimes reaching 100 to 120 pounds. Though authorities differ on the amount of fat in various species, there's no question that chinook are the fattiest and

SALMON AND LEEKS IN FILO

A beautiful dish for a dinner party. Serve it with the sauce described below.

12 tablespoons butter, softened
½ cup lemon juice
2 tablespoons chopped fresh mint (or
    1 teaspoon dried dill)
    Salt and pepper
2 pounds leeks
2 pounds salmon fillets, skinned
½ pound filo dough
1 cup melted butter

1. Whip 8 tablespoons of the butter in processor until fluffy. Through feeder tube, slowly add the lemon juice. Process until thoroughly blended. Transfer mixture to bowl, stir in mint (or dill) and salt and pepper lightly.
2. Wash leeks thoroughly. Trim off root ends and green parts. Pat dry. Cut crosswise into ¼-inch slices. Sauté in remaining 4 tablespoons butter over low heat until leeks are very tender, about 20 minutes.
3. Pat salmon dry. Cut thick parts crosswise into 1½-inch slices. (Thickness and width of portions should be about the same.) Reserve thinner tail ends for another use. You should have eight portions.
4. Defrost filo (if frozen) by allowing to sit in refrigerator at least 2 days. Unroll defrosted filo onto waxed paper and immediately cover with damp (not wet) towel. Let stand for 10 minutes to soften.
5. Uncover filo, remove one sheet and cover again. Lay sheet on flat surface and brush top with melted butter. Remove second sheet, place on first and brush with melted butter. Spread one-eighth of the leeks in the shape of a salmon slice on the filo about one-quarter of the way down the sheet. Lay salmon slice on leeks. Salt and pepper salmon to taste. Spread lemon-butter mixture on salmon.
6. Fold short end of filo over salmon. Then fold sides over to make envelope. Brush top surfaces of filo with melted butter as you go. Roll salmon-stuffed end down sheet over and over to wrap thoroughly. As you roll, brush top of roll each time with melted butter, making certain that salmon ends up at top of packet and leeks at bottom. Trim filo as necessary to end up with the seam on the bottom of the packet. Brush seam with melted butter.
7. Packets may be refrigerated for several hours. Bring them to room temperature before baking.
8. On buttered baking sheet, bake packets at 450°F for 15 minutes. Serve immediately with sauce below.

Serves 8

Sauce

1 cup fish stock
3 egg yolks
½ cup cream
12 tablespoons butter, softened
    Salt and pepper
1 tablespoon lemon juice

1. Reduce fish stock to ¼ cup by simmering. Cool.
2. Combine egg yolks, cream and reduced stock and beat until blended. Over low heat and stirring constantly, cook mixture until it is thick enough to coat the back of a wooden spoon. Do not boil.
3. Off heat, whisk in butter 1 tablespoon at a time. The sauce will thicken considerably.
4. Salt and pepper to taste. Beat in lemon juice. Keep warm over tepid water and serve with filo packets.

Greg Caluya selling salmon at Pike Place Market.

therefore generally the tastiest.

The fat content of any given salmon changes as it goes through its life cycle. Salmon feed in the ocean, storing fat and protein for their journeys upstream to spawn and die. Once they enter fresh water, or approach it, they stop feeding and live off their own bodies. They maintain weight by replacing fat and protein with water. An ocean-caught salmon, therefore, is better than a river-caught fish, especially if it has been caught at the peak of its growth cycle. And fish headed

up longer rivers are likely to be better than fish whose spawning grounds are in short rivers, since the former must be in better shape for their long journey.

A prime chinook born in a long river, then, can attain a fat content of up to 16 percent, twice as much as that of a coho, the next-largest and next-fattiest species.

At their prime, all salmon are pink- or red-fleshed, with the exception of chinook. Chinook vary in color depending on where they are from and other genetic factors. They can be deep red, bright orange,

MINCED SALMON IN LETTUCE CUPS

This variation of a classic Chinese recipe substitutes salmon for chicken.

> 1 pound salmon
> Pinch salt
> 1 egg white
> ½ teaspoon cornstarch
> 1 tablespoon vegetable oil
> 4-5 dried Chinese black mushrooms (or shiitake)
> 1 head iceberg lettuce
> 2 cups oil for deep frying
> ½ cup ground pork
> 2 scallions, minced
> 2 water chestnuts, chopped finely
> ½ cup chicken stock
> ½ tablespoon cornstarch
> 1 tablespoon water

Sauce

> 1 tablespoon sherry
> 2 tablespoons Chinese oyster sauce
> 1 tablespoon soy sauce
> ½ teaspoon sugar
> Pinch salt
> Pinch pepper

1. Process salmon to mince. Combine with salt, egg white, ½ teaspoon of cornstarch and 1 tablespoon vegetable oil. Set aside for 10-15 minutes.
2. Soak mushrooms in hot water 20-30 minutes. Drain and chop coarsely.
3. Form lettuce cups by trimming stalk-end of lettuce, removing large leaves and trimming with scissors into 4- to 5-inch circles.
4. Heat 2 cups vegetable oil in wok or deep pan to 300°F. Add salmon mixture, stirring to separate, for barely 1 minute. Remove and drain.
5. Pour off all oil except 3 tablespoons. Stir-fry pork over medium-high heat until done, breaking up with fork as it cooks. Add scallions and stir-fry 30 seconds. Add mushrooms and water chestnuts and stir-fry another 30 seconds.
6. Add salmon mixture, chicken stock and sauce and toss as it heats through.
7. Dissolve ½ tablespoon cornstarch in 1 tablespoon water. Stir into salmon mixture until thickened. Cook 1 minute more.
8. Spoon mixture into lettuce cups and serve immediately.

Serves 4-6

KOGANE-YAKI

Chef Hide Obatake of the Mikado restaurant in Seattle learned this dish, which means "gold broiled" in English, from another Japanese chef when Obatake first came to this country in the 1960s. It's not classic Japanese, Obatake notes, but it's simple, beautiful and delicious, all virtues in Japanese cooking.

> 1 medium onion, sliced thinly
> 1 cup thinly sliced mushrooms
> Vegetable oil
> 4 salmon fillets
> 3 egg yolks
> 1 cup vegetable oil
> Salt and pepper

1. Sauté onion and mushrooms lightly in a little vegetable oil until limp.
2. Cut four 12-inch squares of aluminum foil and oil tops. Scatter onion and mushrooms in middle of each foil square and place salmon fillets on top, skin side down.
3. Whip egg yolks and cup of vegetable oil to foamy stage. Salt and pepper to taste. Spoon sauce over the fillets. Fold and seal foil packets securely and place in baking pan.
4. Bake in 550°F oven 10-15 minutes, depending on thickness of fillets. Place packets on plates for guests to open. Serve with lemon wedges.

Serves 4

mottled or even white. The latter, the result of a little-understood genetic quirk, are known as "white kings." Fishermen usually receive lower prices for them, but fish markets and restaurants often charge more, evidence that opinions vary as to whether or not white kings are superior.

Less oily than chinook, coho nevertheless have their gastronomic advocates. They can attain weights of 20 pounds, but most run less than half that, making them easier to handle in the kitchen. So-called "baby" coho of a pound or so are reared in pens and resemble trout in taste.

Sockeye, once exclusively canned because of their attractive red flesh, are now found whole in the market on occasion. Their fat content is about the same as that of ocean coho, but most sockeye are river-caught and tend to be drier than coho when cooked.

Pink salmon caught in the ocean can be fat and tasty. But again, most are river-caught and poorly handled because they are netted en masse. They soften quickly and don't hold up very well between boat and market.

Its common name, dog, popularly marks the chum salmon as the lowliest of the Pacific species, thought to be fit only for the Indians' dogs. The name actually refers to the chum's prominent teeth at spawning time. Low in fat and mild in flavor, a chum is edible only if it has bright scales and dark pink flesh.

When buying salmon, follow several rules. First, check that the scales are intact. Missing scales mean that a fish has been abused in handling and likely has tainted flavor. Next, inspect the skin for color. A prime salmon will have a bright bluish back, gleaming silvery sides and a white belly. Dullness and darkness mean that a salmon was caught on the downside of its life cycle.

Now open the fish and inspect the cavity. Flesh should be bright, with a translucent quality. And it should be firm, with no sign of ribs pulling away. Soft flesh, loose ribs and discoloration mean the fish has suffered "belly burn" from not being cleaned properly or immediately. Belly burn results from the powerful acids of a salmon's stomach eating through the stomach wall. Check also to see that the cavity is free of blood, which spoils taste. Run your finger inside the belly; a prime fish will have an oily feel. Finally, the fish should have a natural aroma; a pronounced fishy odor means that decomposition has begun to set in.

Frozen salmon are trickier to judge. Check the scales. Look for belly burn and blood inside the cavity. Make sure the cavity is rounded and the belly has a puffy look. A frozen salmon with a flat belly is one that had dehydrated or had begun to oxidize its fat before freezing. Most frozen salmon is sold thawed. If you buy one still frozen, thaw it slowly in the refrigerator on a rack above a pan so that the fish does not sit in water.

Once you've located a prime salmon, it would be a shame to maltreat it in the kitchen. A common error is overcooking. One way to avoid that is to follow the long-established rule of cooking salmon, by whatever method: 10 minutes per inch as measured at the fish's thickest point. A two-inch-thick salmon cooked on both sides, for instance, should receive 10 minutes of cooking on each side. A baked or poached fish of that size should be cooked for 20 minutes.

SALMON RAVIOLI

Serve these with a sauce of melted butter and a touch of grated Parmesan.

Filling

4 shallots, minced
½ teaspoon minced garlic
4 tablespoons butter
4 cups cooked and flaked salmon
1 tablespoon minced mint
1 tablespoon lemon juice
  Salt and pepper
1 egg plus 1 egg yolk
½ cup ricotta
½ cup grated Parmesan

1. Sauté shallots and garlic in butter over low heat 8-10 minutes without browning. Cool.
2. Combine flaked salmon, mint, lemon juice and salt and pepper to taste. Lightly beat egg and yolk, and beat in ricotta and Parmesan to blend. Combine shallots and garlic with salmon and egg mixtures gently so as not to break up salmon. Refrigerate until ready to use.

Pasta

3 cups unbleached flour
3 large eggs
3 teaspoons olive oil
  Salt

1. Mound flour on board. Make well in mound and break eggs into well. Add oil and a little salt. Mix well with fork, then incorporate flour little by little from lower part of inner ring. When half the flour is absorbed, begin kneading with hands until almost all flour is absorbed.
2. If using pasta machine, follow instructions and roll out sheets as thin as possible. If making by hand, knead dough 10 minutes then roll out as thin as possible with a pin on a floured board. (Divide dough into 3 balls and roll out each separately.)

3. Form ravioli while pasta is still moist. Place ½-tablespoon mounds of filling about 2 inches apart on sheet of pasta. Cover with another sheet and use ravioli cutter, making sure edges of each filled envelope are sealed.
4. Drop ravioli in boiling, salted water. When they rise to surface, cook about 1 minute, testing for doneness. Remove with slotted spoon.

Serves 6-8

SALMON STEAKS WITH MINT-TOMATO SAUCE

The mint transforms this tomato cream sauce into something special.

1½ cups cream
3 shallots, minced
5 tablespoons butter
½ cup white wine
½ cup fish stock
4 tomatoes, peeled, seeded and chopped coarsely
2 tablespoons minced fresh mint
1 teaspoon lemon juice
  Salt and pepper
4 salmon steaks, 1 inch thick

1. Reduce cream by simmering to ¾ cup.
2. Saute shallots in 2 tablespoons of the butter over medium heat 2-3 minutes. Add wine and fish stock and boil 5 minutes. Add tomatoes and cook, stirring, until juice has evaporated, about 5 minutes.
3. Add reduced cream, 1 tablespoon of the mint, lemon juice and salt and pepper to taste. Set aside.
4. In large skillet, melt remaining 3 tablespoons of butter and saute salmon 4-5 minutes on each side. (Salmon should be slightly underdone.) Remove excess butter from skillet. Add sauce and heat through. Sprinkle with remaining mint and serve immediately.

Serves 4

Poached
Salmon with
Basil Sauce

Smoked
Salmon
Gratin

POACHED SALMON WITH BASIL SAUCE

The sauce can be done in advance for this dish. Simply lay a buttered circle of waxed paper on the surface and set aside for up to 3 hours. Before serving, whisk the sauce over low heat until it is quite warm, but do not boil.

Basil Sauce

> ½ cup fish stock
> 2 tablespoons butter
> 2 tablespoons minced scallion
> 1 bunch basil, chopped coarsely
> 5 tablespoons white wine vinegar
> 5 tablespoons white wine
> ¾ pound unsalted butter, heated to 160-180°F
> 1 tablespoon lemon juice
> Salt and pepper

1. Reduce fish stock by boiling to 2 tablespoons.
2. Sauté scallions in 2 tablespoons butter over low heat 3-4 minutes. Add basil and cook, stirring, until limp. Add vinegar, wine and reduced fish stock. Simmer until liquid becomes syrupy.
3. Puree basil mixture in processor until smooth. With machine running, add heated butter steadily in a thin stream. Season with lemon juice and salt and pepper to taste. Set sauce aside and reheat or keep warm while fish is poaching by placing in a container of hot water.

Poached Salmon

> 4 quarts water
> ⅓ cup white wine vinegar
> 1 tablespoon salt
> 3 scallions, chopped
> 1 stalk celery, chopped
> 6 salmon steaks

1. Boil water and other ingredients (except salmon) 5 minutes. Add salmon steaks and cook at barest simmer for about 8 minutes, or until salmon is done.
2. Puddle sauce on serving plates, top with salmon steaks, spoon more sauce on top and garnish with basil leaves. Serve immediately.

Serves 6

SMOKED SALMON GRATIN

Smoked salmon is almost as plentiful in Washington as fresh. Here is a dish that uses the less expensive hard-smoked kind.

> ¼ cup minced onion
> 4 tablespoons butter
> ½ pound button mushrooms, quartered
> 3 tablespoons flour
> 1 cup milk, boiling
> ¼ cup white wine
> ¼ teaspoon dried dill
> Salt and pepper
> 6 tablespoons cream
> 1½ cups hard-smoked salmon, flaked
> ¼ cup grated Swiss or Gruyère cheese
> 1 tablespoon butter

1. Sauté onion in butter over low heat 4-5 minutes. Turn up heat to medium. Add mushrooms and sauté 10-12 minutes, until their liquid has evaporated. Stir in flour. Cook, stirring, about 2 minutes, until the flour disappears.
2. Off heat, stir in boiling milk, wine, and dill. Salt and pepper to taste. Return to heat and, stirring, boil 3-4 minutes to thicken. Add cream to thin. Fold in salmon.
3. Spread mixture in buttered baking dish or scallop shells. Sprinkle with grated cheese and dot with butter. Bake at 425°F for about 15 minutes, until top is browned.

Serves 4-6

BAKED SALMON WITH TOMATO COULIS

This is one of the standard Washington methods for baking a whole salmon. When tomatoes are at their prime, the coulis is a perfect sauce.

>   1 whole salmon, 8-10 pounds
>   Salt and pepper
>   ¼ cup lemon juice
>   ¼ cup butter, melted
>   1 lemon, sliced to ¼-inch thickness
>   1 onion, sliced to ½-inch thickness

Basting Sauce:

>   ½ cup water
>   ¼ cup white wine
>   2 tablespoons butter

1. Rub cavity of fish with lemon juice. Sprinkle with salt and pepper. Let stand at room temperature for about 30 minutes.
2. Line pan with buttered foil. Brush fish with melted butter on both sides and place on foil. Stuff cavity with lemon and onion slices.
3. Bake in a 425°F oven 35-40 minutes, or until thermometer stuck in thickest part of fish registers 125°F. Make basting sauce by bringing ingredients to boil and simmering 5 minutes. Baste salmon 2 or 3 times while it is cooking.

Serves 10-12

Tomato Coulis

>   ½ cup minced shallots
>   3 cloves garlic, minced
>   4 tablespoons butter
>   8 ripe tomatoes, peeled, seeded and
>   chopped
>   1 cup fresh basil, cut in strips
>   ½ cup olive oil
>   2 tablespoons red wine vinegar
>   Salt and pepper

1. Saute shallots and garlic in butter until tender but not browned. Add tomatoes and saute at high heat for 5 minutes. Reduce heat to medium and simmer for 10-15 minutes, until most of the liquid has evaporated. Remove from heat.
2. Add basil, olive oil and vinegar. Salt and pepper to taste. Then puree in food processor.
3. Reheat and serve. (Or serve at room temperature with cold fish.)

SALMON SAUCE FOR PASTA

What do you do with leftover baked, poached or grilled salmon? You can try this simple sauce.

>   ½ cup fish stock or clam juice
>   ¼ cup white wine
>   6 tablespoons butter
>   3 cups cream
>   2 cups cooked salmon, flaked
>   ¼ cup shredded fresh mint (or
>   1 tablespoon dried dill)
>   Salt and white pepper
>   1 pound fresh linguine or fettuccine

1. Combine fish stock or clam juice with wine and 3 tablespoons of the butter. Bring to boil and reduce to ⅓ cup.
2. Simmer cream until reduced by one-third. Combine with stock. Add salmon and mint or dill. Salt and pepper to taste. Remove from heat and keep warm.
3. Cook pasta in boiling, salted water. Drain and toss with the remaining 3 tablespoons of butter.
4. Toss pasta with the sauce. Serve on heated plates and garnish with shredded mint leaves.

Serves 4-6

Baked
Salmon with
Tomato
Coulis

Salmon
Sauce for
Pasta

BRAISED SALMON

Tripo Costello's principal claim to fame is his annual portrayal of Santa Claus on the Bellingham Christmas Ship. But this former construction man and commercial fisherman of Slovenian descent also is a renowned cook, especially of fish. This recipe is adapted from his careful advice.

3- to 4-pound chunk of salmon, bone in
   2 cloves garlic, chopped finely
   1 stalk celery, chopped
   1 large onion, chopped
   ½ cup chopped parsley
   4 tablespoons olive oil
   2 cups white wine
   2 bay leaves
   1 8-ounce can tomatoes, chopped
   1 small can tomato sauce
   Salt and pepper

1. Remove scales from salmon and clean thoroughly.
2. In fish poacher or other covered pan large enough to hold salmon, sauté garlic, celery, onion and parsley in olive oil over low heat until vegetables are wilted, 6-8 minutes. Add wine, bay leaves, tomatoes and tomato sauce. Salt and pepper to taste. Simmer 20 minutes.
3. Place salmon in sauce, cover and simmer 60-90 minutes. Regulate heat so that sauce is at barest simmer. Add water if needed to maintain sauce's consistency.
4. Serve salmon with sauce on the side.
Serves 4-6

CREAM OF SALMON SOUP

Here's a soup elegant enough for the dining room and hearty enough for the patio.

   1 quart fish stock (or clam juice)
   ¼ cup butter
   ⅓ cup flour
   ½ cup crème fraiche (see Notes on
      Ingredients, page xi)
   1 cup cream
   1 tablespoon tomato paste
   Salt and pepper
   ½ pound salmon fillets, skinned
   1 medium tomato, peeled, seeded and
      cut in ¼-inch cubes
   ¼ cup fresh basil (if not fresh, omit)
   1 tablespoon chopped chives

1. Bring stock or clam juice to boil. Make roux by melting butter over low heat. When it stops foaming, beat in flour. Cook 2 minutes, stirring. Add clam juice or stock to the roux and bring back to a boil, stirring constantly. Reduce heat and simmer 10-15 minutes.
2. Combine crème fraiche, cream and tomato paste. Add ½ cup hot stock or clam juice to mixture and stir. Add mixture to remaining hot clam juice or stock. Salt and pepper to taste.
3. Cube salmon in ½-inch chunks. Add to soup along with tomato and basil. Reheat soup for 5-7 minutes, until salmon is cooked, but do not boil. Sprinkle with chives and serve.
Serves 4

SALMON SOUP
WITH AIOLI

Unlike the previous recipe, this soup is not made with cream. But it's just as good.

3 pounds salmon fillets, skinned
2 cloves garlic, minced
1 onion, chopped finely
¼ cup olive oil
1 cup canned tomatoes, drained and
    chopped coarsely
6 cups clam juice (or fish stock)
⅓ cup white wine
    Pinch red pepper flakes
2 tablespoons tomato paste
    Salt and pepper
6 croutons (see note below)
    Aioli (see below)

1. Cut salmon into 2-inch cubes.
2. Sauté garlic and onion in olive oil over low heat 10-12 minutes until limp. Add tomatoes and sauté 3 minutes more. Add all other ingredients except salmon, croutons and aioli, and simmer 30 minutes.
3. Add salmon, bring soup to boil, reduce heat and simmer 5 minutes, until salmon is just cooked.
4. Place croutons on heated soup plates, ladle on soup, garnish with generous dollop of aioli and serve hot.

Serves 6

Aioli

Here's just one method of preparing this classic sauce from southern France.

1 tablespoon dried bread crumbs
1 tablespoon red wine vinegar
6 cloves garlic, chopped
3 egg yolks
2 tablespoons lemon juice
½ teaspoon salt
½ teaspoon pepper
1½ cups olive oil

1. Soak bread crumbs in vinegar. Squeeze liquid from crumbs. Combine crumbs with all other ingredients except olive oil in processor. Process 1 minute.
2. With machine running, add oil in thin but steady stream and process until blended. Refrigerate in container with tight-fitting cover.

Note: *To make croutons, slice French or Italian bread, butter slices (or drizzle with olive oil) and toast in a 325°F oven until lightly browned.*

BROILED SALMON WITH
HERB SAUCE

Quick and simple, this works for broiling in the house or grilling outdoors.

10 leaves fresh mint, chopped finely
5 large basil leaves, chopped finely
2 tablespoons soy sauce
2 tablespoons lemon juice
⅓ cup olive oil
    Salt and pepper
4 salmon steaks or fillets

1. Mix all ingredients except salmon and marinate salmon in mixture at room temperature for 1 hour.
2. Drain salmon, reserving marinade. Broil or grill salmon, being careful not to overcook.
3. Meanwhile, warm marinade and serve with salmon.

Serves 4

BRANDADE OF SALMON

Brandade is a French dish of salt cod pounded with garlic and oil. Here's a Washington version using salmon combined with russet potatoes. Serve it as a first course or light meal.

    1 pound russet potatoes
    ¼ small onion, chopped
    1 tablespoon butter
    ½ cup white wine
    2 cups fish stock (or clam juice)
    1 pound salmon fillets, skinned and
        cubed
    ½ cup olive oil
    ½ cup cream
    1 tablespoon mashed garlic
    Salt and pepper

1. Boil potatoes in their jackets until tender, peel and pass through ricer or food mill.
2. Sauté onion in butter over low heat until limp, 6-8 minutes. Add wine, increase heat and boil to reduce by one-half. Add stock and bring to boil again. Add salmon, reduce heat and simmer until barely cooked, about 5 minutes. Drain and reserve 1 cup of the poaching liquid for mustard sauce (see below).
3. While salmon cooks, warm olive oil and cream in separate pans.
4. When salmon is cooked and drained, process until smooth. Add garlic. With machine running, add warm oil and enough warm cream to make a puree the consistency of slightly thickened cream. (Add more cream if necessary to achieve proper consistency.) Add potatoes and process until just blended. Salt and pepper to taste. Transfer to top of double boiler and keep warm on stove while preparing the sauce. Serve warm with mustard sauce.

Serves 6-8.

Mustard Sauce

    ¼ small onion, minced
    1 tablespoon butter
    ½ cup white wine
    1 cup reserved salmon poaching liquid
    1½ cups cream
    Salt and pepper
    1 tablespoon butter, cut into bits
    4 teaspoons coarse-grained mustard

1. Sauté minced onion in butter over low heat 5 minutes. Add wine, increase heat and boil to reduce by half. Add salmon poaching liquid and boil to reduce by half. Add cream, reduce heat and simmer to reduce by half. Strain.
2. Salt and pepper to taste. Return to heat and whisk in butter bit by bit. Whisk in mustard and serve warm.

STONE FRUITS

STONE FRUITS

Washington's worldwide identification with apples obscures the state's bountiful production of other tree fruits. Washington residents, however, well know that the tree-fruit season begins long before the apple harvest.

Sweet cherries, for instance, fresh from the Tri-Cities and Wenatchee areas, begin arriving in markets about the second week of June. They are the first of those summer delectables known as stone fruits. With a couple of exceptions, Washington does not rank among the leading producers of stone fruits. But, oh, those exceptions!

Foremost among them are the sweet cherries. Washington leads the nation in producing sweet cherries, growing from a third to a half of the nation's output each year, depending on weather conditions.

Ah, the weather. Central Washington's mild, dry climate is ideal for growing sweet cherries—when the weather's normal. Washington can produce 70,000 to 80,000 tons of sweet cherries in a good year. But a late frost or early summer rains will devastate cherries, which absorb water through their skins, and sometimes, alas, that happens.

That hasn't seemed to discourage Washington's cherry growers. They have increased their production sevenfold in the past 30 years, to some 10,000 acres. Most of that production is sold fresh, with only about 15 percent of the crop being held out for canning, freezing and processing into candied and maraschino cherries.

Washington's dominant cherry is the dark-red Bing, which constitutes some 60 percent of the state's production. Second (20 percent of the crop) is a close cousin, the Lambert, which follows the Bing to market since it grows at higher elevations and thus is harvested later. Lamberts are nearly indistinguishable from Bings, although Lamberts are slightly more heart-shaped and contain slightly smaller pits.

Of the remaining sweet varieties grown in Washington, the most noticeable is the Rainier, developed in the state and first planted in the mid-1960s. The Rainier is a large, extremely sweet cherry of dramatic coloration: white with a golden pink-to-red blush. Rainiers are more expensive than other varieties both because of demand and because they are so delicate they require much hand labor to harvest. Rainier trees also require four pickings, as the fruit gradually ripens, compared to one picking for Bings.

Growing and, especially, harvesting conditions markedly affect the flavor and sweetness of cherries. Unfortunately, it's not always easy to select the choicest by looks alone. Green stems, as opposed to brown, however, are a tip-off that cherries

CHERRY CAKE

Here is a version of a famous cake from the Basque region of France and Spain. It is especially good when served warm.

> 1 pound sweet cherries, pitted
> ½ cup water
> ½ cup sugar

Pastry

> 2½ cups flour
> 1 cup sugar
> 1 egg
> 2 egg yolks
> Pinch salt
> 14 tablespoons chilled butter, cut into bits
> Zest of 1 lemon

1. Combine cherries, water and sugar and simmer 20-25 minutes, stirring occasionally, until cherries are tender. Briefly process mixture or pass through food mill. Return to stove and cook over medium-high heat, stirring, until mixture is as thick as jam. Cool.
2. Prepare pastry by mixing flour and sugar. Beat egg and egg yolks with salt. Stir eggs into flour mixture.
3. Knead butter and lemon zest into dough. Continue kneading dough until smooth. Form into ball and chill in refrigerator 1 hour.
4. Pat two-thirds of the chilled dough into the bottom and up the sides of buttered 8- or 9-inch cake pan. Fill with cherry mixture. Roll out remaining dough and lay over cherry mixture, pinching top and sides of dough with fingers to seal. Slit top several times with the point of a knife.
5. Bake at 350°F for 45 minutes, then reduce heat to 300°F and bake 20-30 minutes more. Cool at least 30 minutes before serving.

Serves 6-8

CHERRY CRISP

The addition of ground almonds and the cream topping makes this sumptuous enough to serve company.

> 4 cups sweet cherries, pitted
> 1 tablespoon lemon juice
> ½ cup flour
> ½ cup brown sugar
> ½ cup ground blanched almonds
> ½ cup butter, chilled

Topping

> ½ cup sour cream
> ½ cup cream
> Sugar

1. Toss cherries with lemon juice and spread in 9-inch pie pan.
2. Mix flour, brown sugar and ground almonds. Working quickly, cut in chilled butter with pastry blender or fingertips until mixture is mealy. Spread over cherries.
3. Bake at 375°F for 30-35 minutes.
4. Prepare topping by whipping creams together, with sugar to taste, until slightly thickened. Serve over hot or cold cherry crisp.

Serves 4-6

Elsie Patterson of Dixie spooning out cherries.

haven't been stored and thus are likely to be in better condition. Skin color, the darker the better for Bings and Lamberts, reveals whether or not the cherries have been allowed to mature on the trees.

Sweet cherries are best enjoyed uncooked. Nevertheless, there are many ways to use them in the kitchen.

The other stone fruit with a special affinity for Washington is the plum variety known as Italian Prune. Washington leads the nation in the production of Italian Prune plums. That's a limp distinction, however, since the state grows only 15,000

tons of Italian Prunes annually, a drop in California's huge plum bucket.

Most California plums are the types that are best eaten fresh, too sweet and juicy for cooking. The Italian Prune, on the other hand, is superb for cooking. For one thing, being freestone, it's easy to work with. For another, it's not too juicy, and its tart-sweet yellow flesh picks up color from the skin during cooking, turning it to an appetizing crimson.

Washington's commercial Italian Prune plum business is located almost entirely within the Yakima Valley, although

PICKLED CHERRIES

These should be left to mature for several weeks before eating.

2 pounds sweet cherries
4 cups white wine vinegar
1 pound light brown sugar
6 whole cloves
Peel of 1 lemon
1 stick cinnamon

1. Rinse and dry cherries. Pack them into sterilized canning jars.
2. In a noncorrosive pan, combine vinegar with sugar. Bring to boil and simmer 5 minutes. Add remaining ingredients and simmer 10 minutes more. Cool. Strain and pour over fruit, making certain all fruit is completely covered. Can according to your normal procedure.

BRANDIED CHERRIES

Here's another method of preserving cherries. Only these should be left to mature for at least several months, if not a year. The cherries probably won't be worth eating, having given up their flavor to the liqueur. But, oh, the liqueur!

Sweet cherries
Sugar
Brandy

1. Rinse and dry cherries. Prick them several times, then place them in jars or crocks with tight-fitting lids or stoppers. Pour in sugar to reach about one-quarter of the way up, then fill with brandy.
2. Screw on lids or force in stoppers and store in a cool, dry place. Turn containers gently from time to time as cherry liqueur matures, to help dissolve sugar.

CHERRY ICE CREAM

This is a freezer type of ice cream, packed with cherry flavor. To make a finer-textured ice cream, add another beating-freezing step before serving. Freezer ice cream should be eaten within a day or so of preparation.

2½ cups pitted sweet cherries
1½ teaspoons gelatin
¼ cup cold water
2 cups milk
1 cup sugar
Pinch salt
2 tablespoons lemon juice
2 cups cream

1. Briefly process cherries into pulp, or pass through food mill. (You'll need about 1½ cups of pulp.)
2. Mix gelatin with cold water. Combine milk, sugar and salt and bring to boiling point. Remove from heat and stir in gelatin. Cool.
3. Stir cherry pulp and lemon juice into cooled milk mixture. Pour mixture into freezer trays and chill until slushy.
4. Whip slush until thick but not stiff. Whip cream until thick but not stiff. Combine cream and cherry slush. Pack ice cream firmly into freezer trays, cover with plastic wrap and chill in freezer 2 hours.
5. After chilling, remove ice cream from trays and beat thoroughly. Repack into trays, recover with plastic wrap and freeze 2-3 hours before serving.

Serves 6-8

Pickled
Cherries

Brandied
Cherries

Cherry Ice
Cream

many Western Washington backyards contain Italian Prune trees. Backyard orchardists know that to reach full flavor, Italian Prunes need to ripen to the point when their stem ends are slightly shriveled and quite soft to the touch. Ripening plums in the kitchen is best accomplished at room temperature. Enclose them in a paper bag to hasten the process, since the bag traps the ripening agent, ethylene gas.

Two other Washington plums are grown commercially in small quantities: Presidents and Friars. Presidents are larger versions of Italian Prunes. Friars are another good cooking plum. They're large, black, amber-fleshed plums and arrive at market a week or so before the Italian Prune's and President's six-week harvest begins in early August.

Back in the days when home canning was widely practiced, Washington had another important stone fruit, the apricot. Nowadays, apricots grown in the state are nearly all fresh-fruit varieties, and annual apricot production has declined in Washington to between 2,000 and 3,000 tons compared to the 15,000 tons of the 1950s. Today, Washington's apricot business is insignificant compared to California's, although Washington does rank second nationally. The principal varieties grown in Washington are Perfection and Patterson. Both are excellent eaten out of hand and can be included in certain cooked dishes.

Look for Washington apricots from early July to mid-August, during the harvest in the Yakima and Wenatchee valleys. Avoid green, hard apricots. Fully ripened, apricots should have a golden blush and give to the touch.

As with apricots, Washington's peach and nectarine crops pale next to some other states'. But Central Washington growers do produce about 15,000 tons of them annually, and the quality of the best exceeds those shipped in from other areas.

CHERRY SOUP

Mark Lanfear, who, with Ken Shore, owns The John Horan House Restaurant in Wenatchee, developed this recipe to take advantage of Central Washington's fruit production. Lanfear and Shore keep their menu attuned to the changing harvest and substitute Italian Prune plums for the sweet cherries in the soup when the plum season arrives. While the recipe below calls for shrimp stock, a good chicken stock may be used instead.

> 1 medium onion, chopped finely
> 2 cloves garlic, minced
> 4 tablespoons butter
> ⅓ cup flour
> ½ cup sherry
> ½ cup honey
>   Freshly grated nutmeg
> 3 cups sweet cherries (or Italian Prune plums), pitted and chopped
> 5 cups shrimp stock (see below)
> 1½ cups crème fraiche (see Notes on Ingredients, page xi)
>   Salt and pepper

Garnish

> ½ cup crème fraiche
> ½ cup additional chopped fruit
>   Fresh mint

1. In large soup pot, sauté onion and garlic in butter over medium heat until translucent, 5-7 minutes. Slowly sift flour into pot, whisking constantly, and cook 1-3 minutes. Stir in sherry and honey. Grate in nutmeg to taste, about 4 gratings. Stir in cherries or prune plums. Cook 1-2 minutes.
2. Add stock, bring almost to a boil, reduce heat and simmer 30 minutes. Slowly stir in crème fraiche. Bring back to simmer but don't allow to boil. Salt and pepper to taste.
3. Garnish with a dollop of creme fraiche in the center of each portion, sprinkle some of the additional fresh fruit on the crème fraiche and lay a mint leaf alongside. Serve hot.

Serves 6-8

Shrimp Stock

> 6 cups shrimp shells
> 1 tablespoon whole black peppercorns
> 2 garlic cloves, slightly crushed
> 3 quartered onions, skins on
> 2 cups peeled and chopped carrots
>   Small handful parsley
> 5 cups water
> 1 cup white wine
> 1 tablespoon dried thyme
> 4 bay leaves

Combine all ingredients in pot, bring to boil, reduce heat and simmer 3 hours, skimming occasionally. (Add water as necessary to keep ingredients covered.) Strain, first through sieve and then through cheesecloth. Add water if necessary to make the 5 cups stock called for in soup recipe. (If using chicken stock instead of shrimp, substitute 3 pounds chicken scraps or parts for the shrimp shells and brown chicken in ¼ cup vegetable oil before adding other ingredients.)

POACHED CHERRIES

This easy dessert exploits both the flavor and the deep color of sweet cherries. Serve it with, say, almond cookies.

> 1½ cups water
> ½ cup sugar
> 1½ pounds sweet cherries, pitted
> ½ cup red currant jelly
> 1 teaspoon lemon juice
> 2 tablespoons brandy

1. Bring water to a boil, stir in sugar, add cherries, reduce heat and simmer until cherries are almost tender. Drain, reserving juice for another use.
2. Melt jelly with lemon juice, remove from heat and stir in brandy.
3. Add drained cherries to warm jelly and stir gently. Chill before serving.

Serves 4-6

PLUM RELISH

This Belgian specialty goes perfectly with hot or cold meats or poultry. Keep it in the refrigerator for up to two weeks, freeze it, or can it according to your usual method.

> 3 pounds Italian Prune plums
> 1½ cups red wine
> 1½ cups red wine vinegar
> 2½ cups sugar
> 12 whole cloves
> 1 stick cinnamon

1. Prick plums several times with needle. Place them in glass or ceramic bowl.
2. In a noncorrosive pan, combine remaining ingredients and bring to boil. Reduce heat, cover and simmer 10-12 minutes. Cool.
3. Pour cooled mixture over plums. Let stand overnight at room temperature.
4. The following day, drain the liquid from the plums and bring it to a boil. Cool again.
5. Pour cooled mixture over plums and let stand overnight again at room temperature.
6. The following day, place plums and liquid in noncorrosive pan and cook over low heat until the plum skins begin to tear.
7. Remove plums with slotted spoon. Reduce liquid by boiling until thick. Strain and cool. Pour over plums and refrigerate, freeze or can.

Makes about 4 pints

PLUM TART

This recipe was developed by Angela Owens of Seattle, one of the best, most relaxed cooks we know—good bloodlines, too, being the daughter of Angelo and Virginia Pellegrini, whose expertise is represented elsewhere in this book. Before going into the oven, the tart will be far plumper than it turns out, as the plums give up their juice during baking. It looks as good as it tastes.

Filling

> 1½ pounds Italian Prune plums,
>   halved and pitted
> 2 tablespoons sugar
> 1 teaspoon orange zest
> ½ teaspoon cinnamon
> 1 tablespoon butter

Pastry

> 8 tablespoons unsalted butter, softened
> ¼ cup sugar
>   Pinch salt
> 1 egg yolk
> 1 teaspoon vanilla
> 1 cup plus 2 tablespoons flour

1. Prepare pastry by creaming butter and sugar until light yellow. Beat in salt, egg yolk and vanilla. Stir in flour until well blended. Pat pastry out on lightly floured surface to an 8-inch circle. Carefully place in unbuttered 10-inch springform pan or tart pan with removable rim. Press evenly into pan until pastry is 1½ inches up sides.
2. Overlap plum halves in concentric circles on pastry. Mix sugar, orange zest and cinnamon. Sprinkle over plums. Dot with butter.
3. Bake at 400°F for 15 minutes. Reduce heat to 350°F and bake about 45 minutes more, until plums are tender. Allow to cool at least 30 minutes before opening springform or removing tart-pan ring. Serve with whipped or ice cream.

Serves 6-8

Steamed
Plum
Pudding
with
Bourbon
Sauce

Prune Plum
Cobbler

STEAMED PLUM PUDDING WITH BOURBON SAUCE

Some plum puddings don't contain plums. This one does, and the sauce offers the very soul of the plums.

Plum Puree

> 1 cup water
> ½ cup sugar
> 3 whole cloves
> ½ stick cinnamon
>   Juice of ½ lemon
> 1½ pounds Italian Prune plums, halved

1. Combine all ingredients except plums and bring to boil. Reduce heat and simmer 10 minutes. Add plums and simmer 15 minutes. Drain and reserve pulp. Return liquid to pan and reduce to ½ cup by boiling. Reserve reduced liquid for sauce.
2. Remove cloves and cinnamon stick from pulp. Puree pulp in blender or processor. You'll need 1 cup of puree for pudding.

Pudding

> 1 cup plum puree
> ¾ cup sugar
> 1 teaspoon baking soda
> 1 egg, beaten
> 2 tablespoons butter, softened
> 1 cup flour
> ½ teaspoon cinnamon
> ½ cup raisins
> ½ cup walnuts, chopped

1. Beat plum puree with sugar, baking soda, egg and butter. Sift flour and cinnamon into bowl. Mix in raisins and nuts. Beat plum mixture into dry ingredients.
2. Turn batter into 1-quart buttered pudding mold. Secure lid (or cover with foil secured by string). Place in deep pan. Pour boiling water into pan until it reaches two-thirds up sides of mold. Cover pan and steam pudding over medium-low heat for 2½ hours. Remove mold from pan and let stand 15-20 minutes before unmolding pudding by inverting onto plate. Serve warm with plum sauce.

Bourbon Sauce

> 1⅓ cups packed light brown sugar
> ⅔ cup bourbon
> 8 tablespoons butter
> ½ cup cream
> ½ cup reduced plum poaching liquid
>   Pinch salt
> 1 cup cream, lightly whipped

Bring all ingredients except cream to boil, reduce heat and simmer 1 hour, until thickened. Stir frequently. Remove from heat and stir in lightly whipped cream. Serve warm over pudding. Serves 6-8

PRUNE PLUM COBBLER

Here's a quick and easy way to make use of Italian Prune plums.

> 2 pounds Italian Prune plums, pitted and quartered
> ½ teaspoon cinnamon
> ¼ cup lemon juice
> ¾ cup packed dark brown sugar
> ½ cup flour
>   Pinch salt
> 4 tablespoons cold unsalted butter, cut into bits

1. Butter a shallow 1-quart baking dish and arrange plums in bottom. Sprinkle with cinnamon and lemon juice.
2. Combine sugar, flour and salt. Blend in butter with a fork until mixture becomes granular. Sprinkle over plums. Bake at 350°F for about 30 minutes, until topping browns well and plums are tender.
3. Serve warm with lightly whipped cream or with ice cream.

Serves 4-6

125

PLUM AND ONION SAUCE

Serve this unusual sauce with poultry, pork, ham or lamb.

2 pounds Italian Prune plums
2 medium onions, sliced thinly
2 tablespoons butter
¼ cup sugar
2 cloves garlic, minced
1 tablespoon red wine vinegar
½ cup red wine
3 tablespoons lemon juice
1 tablespoon minced fresh mint
2 teaspoons minced fresh oregano
   (or 1 teaspoon dried)
½ cinnamon stick
1 bay leaf
   Strip of lemon peel
   Salt

1. Halve and pit plums and slice medium-thick crosswise. Sauté plums and onions in butter over medium-low heat 10 minutes, until soft. Add sugar and garlic and cook 4 minutes more. Increase heat to medium, add remaining ingredients except salt and cook 40-45 minutes, until liquid is syrupy.
2. Discard cinnamon stick, lemon peel and bay leaf. Stir thoroughly. Salt to taste. Serve slightly warm or at room temperature.

Makes 4 cups

PEACH MUFFINS

Ruth Ballard, who runs Ballard Ambulance Service in Wenatchee and is the wife of State Rep. Clyde Ballard, developed this recipe to make use of apples. Friends have begged the recipe from her and used other fruits in place of apples. Here, peaches are substituted.

5½ cups flour
4 tablespoons baking powder
8 tablespoons butter
1½ teaspoons salt
¾ cup sugar
   Sugar
   Eggs
   Milk
2 peaches, peeled and chopped coarsely
   Chopped walnuts

1. Mix flour, baking powder, butter, salt and the ¾ cup sugar.
2. To make about a dozen muffins, measure out 2 cups of the flour mixture (you'll have about 6 cups). Mix in additional sugar, depending on the fruit's sweetness, up to ¼ cup. Lightly beat 1 egg with enough milk to make 1 cup. Stir egg-milk mixture into the flour mixture. Stir in one-third of the chopped peaches and some chopped walnuts. (Repeat procedure for remaining flour mixture if you wish to make more muffins, or refrigerate remaining flour mixture and use later.)
3. Spoon dough into greased muffin pans and bake at 400°F for 25 minutes.

BAKED PEACHES WITH ZABAIONE CREAM

With the zabaione cream on hand, this dessert comes together quickly. The recipe calls for amaretti, the Italian cookies, but another type of plain cookie may be substituted.

　3 firm peaches
　14 amaretti, crumbled
　½ cup finely chopped blanched almonds
　6 teaspoons butter
　6 teaspoons sugar
　¼ cup brandy (or liqueur used to flavor zabaione cream)

1. Blanch peaches and peel. Remove pits and enlarge cavities slightly to accommodate stuffing.
2. Place peaches in buttered baking dish, in one layer. Combine amaretti and almonds. Fill cavities with mixture and top with butter and sugar.
3. Bake at 350°F for 20 minutes. Sprinkle peaches with brandy and return to oven 10-15 minutes longer. Serve at room temperature with zabaione.

Serves 6

Zabaione Cream

　6 egg yolks
　⅓ cup sugar
　⅔ cup Marsala or orange-flavored liqueur
　1 cup cream
　2 tablespoons sugar
　3 tablespoons Marsala or liqueur

1. Boil water in the bottom of a double boiler, making certain the top part does not touch the water.
2. Beat egg yolks with the ⅓ cup sugar in a bowl until the sugar is entirely dissolved (this is important) and the mixture becomes light-colored and fluffy. Slowly stir in the Marsala or liqueur. Transfer mixture to the top of the double boiler.
3. Whisk constantly until the mixture thickens to the point that it holds its shape in a spoon, about 5 minutes. Do not allow mixture to boil. Remove from heat and whisk 2-3 minutes to cool. Lay a round of lightly buttered wax paper on surface of mixture and refrigerate 1 hour to cool completely.
4. Whip cream with 2 tablespoons sugar. Stir in Marsala or liqueur. Combine with cooled zabaione. Serve chilled.

SPICED PEACHES

Try these as an accompaniment to baked ham or cold roast chicken.

　12 firm peaches, peeled
　3 cups white wine
　1 cup white wine vinegar
　1 cinnamon stick
　6 whole cloves
　8 whole peppercorns
　　Peel of one lemon
　2 cups sugar

In a noncorrosive pan, combine all ingredients and simmer 10-15 minutes, until peaches may be pierced easily with knife. Remove lemon peel and allow peaches to cool in liquid. Serve at room temperature.
Serves 12

TAJINE OF LAMB
AND APRICOTS

A tajine (or tagine) is a North African stew. The taste of Morocco is evident in this one, with its combination of meat, sweet and fruit.

    3 pounds lamb, trimmed, cut into
        2-inch chunks
    3 tablespoons butter
    2 tablespoons oil
      Pinch of stem saffron
      Salt and pepper
    1 teaspoon ground ginger
    ½ teaspoon cinnamon
    3 tablespoons minced onion
    1 cup sliced onion
    4 tablespoons honey
    2 pounds fresh apricots, halved and pitted

1. In heavy casserole, brown lamb lightly in 2 tablespoons of the butter combined with the oil, saffron, salt and pepper to taste, ginger, half the cinnamon and the minced onion.
2. Add water to about halfway up the lamb, bring to boil, cover and simmer for 1¼ hours, adding sliced onion after 1 hour.
3. Add remaining cinnamon and honey and simmer until sauce reduces to about 1 cup. Stir in apricots and remaining butter and heat through. Serve over rice or couscous.

Serves 6

APRICOT PUDDING

This is an Austrian dessert with a Washington touch: ground hazelnuts.

Pastry

    1 teaspoon yeast
    ¼ cup lukewarm milk
    2¼ cups flour
    ¼ cup vegetable oil
    ¼ cup melted butter
    1 egg
      Pinch salt
    1 tablespoon sugar

Topping

    ½ cup butter, chilled
    1 cup flour
    1 cup sugar
    ½ teaspoon vanilla extract
    ¾ cup ground hazelnuts
    1 pound apricots, halved and pitted

1. Dissolve yeast in warm milk. Mix in flour, then add vegetable oil, melted butter, egg, salt and sugar. Mix into ball of dough. Cover dough lightly with plastic wrap and let stand 1 hour.
2. Prepare topping by cutting butter into flour with pastry blender or fingertips until mixture is mealy. Mix in sugar, vanilla and ground hazelnuts.
3. Roll out dough to cover a 9-inch tart pan with a removable rim. Press dough into flutes on rim and trim along top.
4. Arrange apricot halves, cut side down, on dough and sprinkle with hazelnut mixture. Bake in a 350°F oven for 40 minutes. Serve warm with lightly whipped cream.

Serves 6

WALLA WALLAS

W alla Walla Sweets. Even the name pleases. Onions so mild and juicy that some aficionados eat them like apples. Onions so popular that their production and consumption has more than doubled during the past 10 years.

This is the era of designer food, when it's every farmer's, packer's and processor's dream to have his name affixed to his product, even as Calvin Klein labeled America's hips. For the 50 or so onion growers in the Walla Walla Valley, that dream has come true. They formed an organization called the Walla Walla Sweet Onion Commission (less official than it sounds) and sell their extraordinary onions complete with a registered trademark.

Washington eagerly awaits the appearance of Walla Walla Sweets each year in June, and the succulent orbs carry the message of this state's bounty up and down the West Coast and into East Coast markets, as well. Even Atlanta welcomes Washington's prized onion, despite the proximity of Walla Walla Sweets' principal rival, the Vidalia sweet onion of Georgia.

Walla Walla Sweets, like other onions, are members of a family that includes hyacinths, lilies, leeks, shallots and chives. The edible cousins of this family have been prized throughout human history. Within the family, Walla Walla Sweets are special.

An aura of mystery surrounds them. Some history and a little chemistry and climatology do no damage to the mystique and explain much.

The history is easy to come by. Walla Walla Sweets have an unofficial historian, Joe J. Locati, a retired inspector for the Federal-State Inspection Service. His Italian immigrant forebears helped bring Walla Walla Sweets to fame.

Onions commonly take the name of their country of origin—Sweet Spanish, for example. On this basis, Locati says, onions coming from southeastern Washington's Walla Walla River Valley should be known as Walla Walla Sweet-French Onions, Italian-Style.

The story goes like this: Around the turn of the century, a French soldier, Peter Pieri, immigrated to the Walla Walla Valley. He brought with him seeds of an Italian onion popular on the French island of Corsica. Some 25 Italian immigrant farmers already were in the valley. They quickly fell for Pieri's delicious onion, which they called the French Onion. What excited them about it was that it was winter-hardy in the valley's mild, somewhat damp climate. Planted in the fall, the onion could survive the cold under an insulating blanket of snow, mature in the spring and be harvested in the summer, several months before Spanish onions, which must be

ONION FOCACCIA

Focaccia is one of Italy's many variations on the pizza theme. Its crust is thicker and more breadlike than pizza's. This one shows off Walla Walla Sweets to advantage. Note that you need a 24-hour head start to prepare the low-fat cheese.

½ cup yogurt
½ cup low-fat ricotta
5 medium Walla Walla Sweets, sliced lengthwise ¼ inch thick
3 tablespoons olive oil
2 eggs
½ cup cream
Salt and pepper
1 tablespoon minced fresh sage (or 1 teaspoon dried)
Focaccia dough (see below)
½ cup grated Parmesan

1. Combine yogurt and ricotta and refrigerate 24 hours to make cheese.
2. Sauté onions in olive oil over low heat until limp, about 20 minutes. Do not allow to brown. Let onions cool to room temperature.
3. Beat eggs, cream and ricotta-yogurt mixture thoroughly. Salt and pepper to taste. Stir in onions and sage.
4. Pour onto dough (see recipe below). Sprinkle with Parmesan. Bake at 400°F for 25 minutes, until browned. Serve immediately.

Serves 4-6

Focaccia Dough

½ package yeast
Pinch sugar
¼ cup hot tap water
1½ cups white flour
Scant ½ cup cold milk
¾ teaspoon salt
1 tablespoon olive oil

1. Dissolve yeast and sugar in hot water. If using food processor, place flour in processor bowl, add yeast mixture and half the milk while machine is turned on. Add salt and oil, then dribble in more milk until soft dough is formed. Let dough rest a few minutes, then process a couple of seconds and turn dough onto lightly floured board. (If not using processor, place yeast mixture and half the milk in bowl, pour in flour, salt and oil and mix by hand, adding milk as needed to make soft dough.)
2. Knead 10 minutes, let rest 2-3 minutes, then knead 5 minutes more, until dough is soft and smooth. Let dough rise in covered and lightly oiled bowl until doubled in bulk, about 90 minutes. Turn out, punch down and let rest, covered, 8-10 minutes.
3. Stretch and roll dough into pizza shape or into rectangle to fit 10-inch-by-15-inch baking pan. Form lip around edge with fingers before pouring on topping.

CREAMED ONIONS

Walla Walla Sweets, cream, a touch of butter and seasonings. Nothing could be simpler or more appropriate for cooking these special onions.

6 cups sliced Walla Walla Sweets
3 tablespoons butter
Nutmeg
Salt and pepper
1 cup cream
Paprika

Sauté onions in butter over low heat 10-12 minutes without browning. Season with a bit of freshly grated nutmeg and salt and pepper to taste. Place onions in buttered baking dish, pour on cream, sprinkle with paprika and bake at 375°F for 30 minutes. Serve hot.

Serves 4-6

John Pao hauling sweet onions.

planted in the spring.

The Italians set out to improve the onion and adapt it to the valley by selective breeding. Within a few years, they were producing large quantities. Officially, the onions were called "yellow globes" until about 20 years ago, when locals began calling them Walla Walla Sweets. The name caught on, and so did the onion. Ten years ago, onion fields covered about 550 acres of the rich valley floor, which also produces wheat, peas, hay, asparagus, spinach and snap beans, and about 400,000 50-pound bags of onions were produced each year. Both those figures have doubled, and now the Walla Walla Gardeners' Association annually ships 10,000 boxes of Walla Walla Sweets.

"Sweets," however, is misleading. The onions' sugar content is negligible. More accurately, if less euphoniously, they should be called "Milds." What distinguishes Walla Walla Sweets from common yellow onions, aside from their large size and softness, is their lack of bite. A sulfurous compound gives onions their harsh, tear-jerking quality. Walla Walla Sweets contain about half as much of this com

TWO ONION SALADS

Since Walla Walla Sweets owe much to Italian immigrants' attention, the following Italian ways with fresh onions are especially appropriate.

Onions and Tomatoes with Basil

> 2 medium Walla Walla Sweets
> 2 medium tomatoes
>   Salt and pepper
>   Extra-virgin olive oil
>   Balsamic vinegar
>   Fresh basil, chopped

Slice onions and tomatoes ¼ inch thick. Overlap slices alternately on platter. Salt and pepper to taste. Drizzle with generous amount of olive oil. Sprinkle with balsamic vinegar to taste. Sprinkle with basil. Let sit at room temperature for 20-30 minutes. Serve. Serves 4-6

Onion and Orange Salad

This combination must be served immediately, before the orange juice cooks the onions. Italians prefer this as a palate-cleanser during a multi-course meal, the way the French serve a sorbet.

> 2 oranges
> 2 medium Walla Walla Sweets
>   Salt and pepper
>   Extra-virgin olive oil
>   Parsley, chopped

Peel oranges and slice very thinly. Slice onions very thinly. Separate into rings. Place oranges on serving plates and scatter with onion rings. Salt and pepper to taste. Drizzle with olive oil, garnish with parsley and serve immediately. Serves 4-6

GRATIN OF ONIONS

Serve this dish for lunch or as a first course for dinner.

> 2 pounds Walla Walla Sweets,
>   diced coarsely
> 2 tablespoons olive oil
> 4 tablespoons butter
> 1 cup tomato strips (see below)
> 2 tablespoons flour
> 3 eggs
> 1 cup cream
> 1 teaspoon minced fresh thyme (or
>   pinch dried)
> ½ cup grated Gruyère cheese
>   Salt and pepper
> ¼ cup grated Parmesan

1. Sauté the onions in olive oil and 3 tablespoons of the butter in a heavy skillet at low heat for about 1 hour, until they are very tender and golden.
2. Prepare tomato strips by peeling, seeding, juicing and pulping tomatoes until only outer shell is left. Cut shells into long strips and cut strips in half.
3. Add tomato strips to the onions. Sprinkle them with flour. Then mix and cook at low heat for 2-3 minutes.
4. Beat eggs and cream together in large bowl. Add onion-tomato mixture, thyme, Gruyère, and salt and pepper to taste.
5. Pour mixture into well-buttered shallow baking dish. Sprinkle with Parmesan and dot with remaining tablespoon of butter.
6. Bake at 375°F in upper third of oven for 30-35 minutes, until puffy and brown. Place briefly under broiler if top needs additional browning. Serve.

Serves 4-6

pound as ordinary yellow onions, and the amount they do contain is diluted by the onions' high water content.

Their juiciness also means that Walla Walla Sweets are not as easily stored as drier onions that are harvested in the fall and sold from storage all winter. Because the season for Walla Walla Sweets is so short, usually from June 20 to August 20, fanciers have invented ingenious methods of preserving them. The most widely admired, if not practiced, of these is to store them in pantyhose. The idea is to drop an onion into the pantyhose, knot the hose above it, drop another one in, tie another knot, and so on. The pantyhose then should be hung in a cool, dry, dark, airy place. Late-harvest onions stored this way should last until Thanksgiving, albeit with harmless sprouts that can be chopped and used like chives to flavor dishes.

Lacking pantyhose, you will find other effective methods, provided the onions are kept apart in a cool, dry area. Spread them on chicken wire, for instance.

Walla Walla Sweets can also be frozen. Steam slices or rings for about three minutes, cool them in a pan over ice (but don't put them in water), then freeze them in small bags. Chopped onions may be frozen without steaming, but they lose their texture in the freezer and generally are suitable only for cooking.

Purists argue, with considerable merit, that the only way to truly enjoy Walla Walla Sweets is to eat them raw, in, say, salads or sandwiches. Cooking Walla Walla Sweets can be successful, however, if they're used in dishes where their lack of bite becomes a virtue and when the proper allowance is made for their unusually high water content.

Finally, seeking out genuine Walla Walla Sweets can be risky since other onions from near Walla Walla also are sold under that name. All *authentic* Walla Walla Sweets, the Walla Walla Sweet Onion Commission swears, are grown from seeds the farmers preserve themselves. Others use commercial seed—a cause for great skepticism among the keepers of the Walla Walla Sweets' tradition. If you can detect a difference, buy only those onions bearing the Commission's logo. It depicts an onion set against the background of the Blue Mountains, which the growers see as they look up from tending their fields.

NORTHWEST ORIENTAL SALAD

This composition salad blends flavors, colors and textures into a dish of Asian beauty and Washington flavor.

> 3 medium Walla Walla Sweets
> 4 medium carrots
> ½ pound sugar snap peas
> 1 can water chestnuts
> 2 cups bean sprouts
> Soy sauce mayonnaise (see below)
> Salt and pepper

1. Quarter onions lengthwise, then slice crosswise ¼ inch thick. Halve carrots lengthwise, then slice thinly on bias. Slice peas into thirds on bias. Drain chestnuts before slicing thinly.
2. Toss cut vegetables with bean sprouts and mayonnaise. Add pepper to taste and salt if necessary.

Soy Sauce Mayonnaise

> 1 clove garlic, minced
> ½ tablespoon minced fresh ginger
> 2 egg yolks
> 3 tablespoons rice wine vinegar
> 3 tablespoons soy sauce
> 2 tablespoons dry sherry
> 1 teaspoon Dijon-style mustard
> 2 teaspoons sugar
> 1½ cups vegetable oil
> ¼ cup sesame oil
> Dash hot pepper sauce
> Salt and pepper

1. Blend garlic, ginger, egg yolks, vinegar, soy sauce, sherry, mustard and sugar for 1 minute in processor.
2. While the machine is still running, dribble in vegetable oil to start and then increase to a steady stream as mayonnaise begins to form. Then add sesame oil.
3. Turn off processor and stir in hot pepper sauce. Salt and pepper to taste.

Serves 6-8

MARINATED ONIONS AND ZUCCHINI

A classic "à la Grecque" preparation, this dish serves as either a first or side course.

> 4 Walla Walla Sweets
> 4 medium zucchini, in ½-inch slices
> Fresh parsley or dill, chopped finely
> Lemon wedges

Marinade

> 1½ cups chicken stock, degreased
> ½ cup white wine
> ½ cup olive oil
> ¼ cup white wine vinegar
> 5 black peppercorns
> 5 coriander seeds
> 2 cloves garlic, sliced
> 2 teaspoons salt
> 3 bay leaves
> ¼ bulb fennel, sliced thinly (or ½ teaspoon fennel seeds)

1. Combine marinade ingredients in pan and bring to boil. Cover and simmer for 30 minutes. Strain, return to pan and taste for salt. (Marinade should be slightly salty.)
2. Peel onions and slice into eighths. Separate into layers.
3. Bring marinade to boil. Add onions and zucchini. Cover and simmer 4-5 minutes, or until just tender, slightly undercooked.
4. Pour into glass bowl and let cool. Refrigerate at least 12 hours. To serve, bring to room temperature, drain vegetables, sprinkle with parsley or dill and garnish with lemon wedges.

Serves 4-6

LAYERED ONION SALAD

Kit Snedaker, food editor of the *Los Angeles Herald-Examiner*, knowledgeable and inventive cook, and witty, loyal friend to the authors, is a Californian by choice. As such, she's a ringer in this book. No matter, her smashing summer salad is too good to be omitted for that reason.

> 10 anchovy fillets, chopped coarsely
> ½ cup chopped black olives
> ½ cup chopped cured olives
> 1 cup chopped fresh mint
> ½ pound feta cheese, rinsed and crumbled
> 4 large Walla Walla Sweets, sliced
> 6 large tomatoes, in eighths, with wedges halved
> 2 cucumbers, halved, seeded and sliced
> 2 red or yellow peppers, halved, seeded and sliced

Dressing

> 1 cup olive oil
> ½ cup red wine vinegar
> 2 cloves garlic, minced
> ½ teaspoon cumin
> Salt and pepper

1. Mix anchovies, olives, mint and feta. Layer, alternately, the onions, tomatoes, cucumbers and peppers, sprinkling each layer with part of the anchovy-olive-cheese mixture.
2. Combine dressing ingredients well, pour over salad, cover and chill overnight.

Serves 6-8

WALLA WALLA SWEET RELISH

Many people first encountered Walla Walla Sweets when they were served this condiment and made to guess, usually unsuccessfully, its main ingredient. "Onions? You're kidding!" A Seattle friend, Carol Barnard, introduced us to it.

> 4 large Walla Walla Sweets, chopped medium fine
> 1 cup cider vinegar
> 1 cup water
> 1 tablespoon sugar
> ⅓ cup mayonnaise
> 1½ tablespoon celery seed
> Salt and pepper

1. Mix onions, vinegar, water and sugar. Cover and refrigerate overnight.
2. Drain onions. Mix with mayonnaise, celery seed and salt and pepper to taste. Serve chilled as condiment to meat, poultry or fish.

Serves 6-8

BAKED ONIONS

Here's a basic method of baking onions that results in a superb accompaniment to any meat from roast beef to barbecued ribs. Baked onions also are tasty served cold.

> Large Walla Walla Sweets, 1 per person
> Olive oil
> Salt
> Balsamic (or red wine) vinegar

1. Carefully remove thin slice from both ends of onions, then quarter them lengthwise. Do not peel them.
2. Place onions in oiled baking pan, brush with oil and sprinkle lightly with salt. Cover with aluminum foil and bake at 350°F for 30 minutes, or until tender.
3. Remove foil, brush again with oil, sprinkle with vinegar and bake 50-60 minutes longer, turning onions several times and basting with pan oil.

INDEX BY TYPE OF DISH

INDEX BY SUBJECT

A

B

142